THE

ARENA AND THE THRONE.

L. T. TOWNSEND, D. D.,

AUTHOR OF "CREDO," "SWORD AND GARMENT," "GOD-MAN," ETC., ETC.

NEW YORK:
NELSON AND PHILLIPS,
805 BROADWAY.

Stereotyped at the Boston Stereotype Foundry,

No. 19 Spring Lane.

TO

MY STEP-FATHER,

ALVIN FLETCHER,

WHOSE KINDNESS TO THE FATHERLESS DESERVES
A LARGER RETURN THAN WE HAVE
POWER TO GIVE,

This Volume

IS AFFECTIONATELY DEDICATED.

PREFACE.

The subjects herein discussed were first treated with no thought of publication. They grew into their present shape while the author was engaged in professional duties in the pulpit and lecture-room. One day they formed a voluntary relationship, looked like a book, were presented to the publishers, and accepted.

If the public receives this volume with the same favor as other books of the author have been received, he will be satisfied.

CONTENTS.

APPENDIX.

THE FIELD.

O, rack me not to such extent;
These distances belong to Thee;
The world's too little for Thy tent,
A grave too big for me. HERBERT.

Thy breath sustains yon fiery dome;
But man is most thy favored home. STERLING.

Behold this midnight splendor, — worlds on worlds;
Ten thousand add and twice ten thousand more,
Then weigh the whole; one soul outweighs them all,
And calls the seeming vast magnificence
Of unintelligent creation poor. YOUNG.

Not to this evanescent speck of earth
Poorly confined; the radiant tracts on high
Are our exalted range; intent to gaze
Creation through, and from that full complex
Of never-ending wonders, to conceive
Of the Sole Being right. THOMSON.

O rich and various man! thou palace of sight and sound, carrying in thy senses the morning, and the night, and the unfathomable galaxy; in thy brain the geometry of the city of God; in thy heart the power of love and the realms of right and wrong. An individual man is a fruit which it costs all the foregoing ages to form and ripen. He is strong, not to do, but to live; not in his arms, but in his heart; not as an agent but as a fact. EMERSON.

Man, if he compares himself with all that he can see, is at the zenith of power; but if he compares himself with all that he can conceive, he is at the nadir of weakness.

COLTON.

Up, man! for what if thou with beasts hast part,
Since in the body framed of dust thou art?
Yet know thyself upon the other side
Higher than angels, and to God allied. TRENCH.

Roll on, ye stars! exult in youthful prime;
Mark with bright curves the printless steps of Time:
Near and more near your beamy cars approach,
And lessening orbs on lessening orbs encroach:
Flowers of the sky! ye, too, to age must yield, —
Frail as your silken sisters of the field!
Star after star from heaven's high arch shall rush,
Suns sink on suns, and systems systems crush,
Headlong, extinct, to one dark centre fall,
And Death, and Night, and Chaos mingle all!
Till o'er the wreck, emerging from the storm,
Immortal Nature lifts her changeful form,
Mounts from her funeral pyre on wings of flame,
And soars and shines, another and the same.

DARWIN.

Ye golden lamps of heaven! farewell,
With all your feeble light;
Farewell, thou ever-changing moon,
Pale empress of the night!
And thou, refulgent orb of day!
In brighter flames arrayed,
My soul, that springs beyond thy sphere,
No more demands thine aid.
Ye stars are but the shining dust
Of my divine abode,
The pavement of those heavenly courts
Where I shall reign with God. DODDRIDGE.

Learn more reverence; not for rank or wealth; that needs no learning;
That comes quickly — quick as sin does! ay, and often leads to sin;
But for Adam's seed — man! Trust me, 'tis a clay above your scorning,
With God's image stamped upon it, and God's kindling breath within. MRS. BROWNING.

THE FIELD.

IS the entire physical universe inhabited or inhabitable, are questions which for two centuries have received, from able disputants, both affirmative and negative answers. As each last writer has closed his argument, he seems to have completely silenced all opponents; but anon is himself silenced by some new comer with hands full of additional data.

The advocates of a Plurality of Inhabited Worlds find in Fontenelle their first and ablest advocate. His efforts at popularizing the discoveries of Newton and the calculations of Kepler, which had just then introduced the system of modern astronomy, were successful. His "Plurality of Worlds," published in 1686, was full of freshness, intelligence, and grace, and has justly won much praise for the author.

Twelve years later, "Cosmotheoros," by Christian Huygens, a Dutchman, — a work which is far less pleasing in style, but far more correct, scientifically, than Fontenelle, -- appeared in Paris. The various other treatises that immediately followed were little else than imitations of Fontenelle and Huygens. The controversy between Sir David Brewster, supporting the idea of inhabited planets, and Mr. Whewell, contradicting it, brought out, in 1833, all the new scientific material then known, which in any way bore upon the subject. The works of Richard A. Proctor have given us the products of the more recent investigations, and are worthy of careful study.*

It will be seen, upon review of the different arguments and speculations presented, that, from first to last, and on both sides, there has been but slight variation in the line of reasoning followed. Arguments from analogy are the favorite ones, especially for those supporting the theory of a plurality of inhabited worlds. The planets resemble the earth, the fixed stars resemble the sun; therefore it is concluded the planets are inhabited, and the fixed stars have attending inhabited planets.

Another argument is drawn from what is regarded as the consistency of things. It is claimed that it ill accords with the goodness, grandeur, and magnificence of the Divine Being, to people this earth with intelligent and moral beings, leaving the surrounding worlds, which are of immensely superior proportions, silent and empty. To say that these arguments, as variously developed and illustrated from year to year, have but little weight, and that they have been easily answered, would be saying what is not true.†

No one can go forth and gaze upon the illimitable

* M. Flammarion, M. Figurier, and a score of men of less note, have, from time to time, written upon the subject, but have, added scarcely anything of importance bearing upon that side of the argument represented by the amusing and ingenious "Conversations" of Fontenelle.

† Appendix A.

heavens with anything like due appreciation of magnitudes, without being well nigh overwhelmed; in such contemplation one feels not like expanding into an angel, but like shrinking into a mote, and is able to find for the emotions excited no fitter expression than the words of inspiration, "When I consider thy heavens, the work of thy fingers, the moon and the stars which thou hast ordained; what is man, that thou art mindful of him, or the son of man, that thou visitest him?"

Replies to the ever-repeated forms of arguments in support of the plurality of inhabited worlds based upon analogy and the consistency of things, have been, from age to age, as uniform as the arguments themselves. Differences between the earth and every known astronomical body have been pointed out, of sufficient magnitude, it has been claimed, to destroy the weight of the argument from analogy; while the force of the argument from consistency, it has been reasoned, depends altogether upon the relative position of humanity in the universe. If man's greatness is not measured by his physical properties, or if to be a man is greater than to be a planet, which certain scientists seem to deny, then this little earth, despite its littleness, may consistently have a place in the divine mind and economy, to which every other planet is an utter stranger.

If the majestic workmanship of God is not confined chiefly to Jupiter and his moons, nor to Saturn and his rings, nor to the magnificence of double stars, nor to the magnitudes of the nebulæ, nor to any of these temporal things, but to *man*, then it is enough, and the consistency of things is sufficiently preserved, even if all these immense astronomical bodies in the universe have no higher or other use save to regulate for man the earth's motions, to aid him in his otherwise perilous navigations, and by study and contemplation to awaken in him thoughts of the skill, power, and grandeur of the Infinite One. And this earth, in its sea, soil, and atmosphere, may be teeming with inhabitants, visible and invisible to the naked eye, simply to show God to man as in an ever-unfolding revelation, which more and more fully dawns upon him at every advancing step of his ceaseless scientific investigations and discovery; and it is possible, also, that not a thing of life is to be found upon any other planet, because they can there serve no such purpose. In fine, it is claimed by those representing this side of the question, that in precisely the proportion that man, by telescopic research and spectroscopic analysis, can make out the physical conditions and proportions of planet, star, or nebula, in that proportion is the end of their creation completely subserved; it is enough, according to this, which we denominate the theological idea, that man can see, not that others must occupy, the planets. Consequently, it is argued that the eyes of the spiritual universe may be fixed upon this earth with an intensity of interest in comparison with which the entire physical universe beside may pale into the merest insignificance.

In addition to this, the theological argument against the plurality of inhabited worlds rarely fails to make its appearance, whenever the subject, from this point of view, is presented. The difficulty, as set forth by this argument, relates to the discrepancy between the theological and the scientific view of the universe. According to theology, this earth, in point of interest, is the centre of the physical universe; it has received a visit in person from the Creator; it has witnessed the union between Deity and humanity; upon it overwhelming interests are represented as culminating; humanity, created in the image of God, springing from one federal head, is working out its probation upon this planet, and upon no other: the eyes of the spiritual universe are accordingly, and almost immovably, fixed upon it; and the hosts of heaven are ministering to its inhabitants.* In fine, it is extremely difficult to overcome the objection of infidelity, that Christianity lavishes altogether too great attentions upon this earth, if it is only one of many similar inhabited worlds. The single point of the divine manifestation in the person of Jesus is to most minds an overwhelming objection, while such a visit and manifestation are per-

* Trench well states the case: "Scripture is no story of the material universe. A single chapter is sufficient to tell us that 'God made the heavens and the earth.' Man is the central figure there; or, to speak more truly, the only figure: all which is there besides serves but as a background for him. He is not one part of the furniture of this planet, not the highest merely in the scale of its creatures, but the lord of all; sun, moon, and stars, and all the visible creation, borrowing all their worth and their significance from the relations where they stand to him. Since he appears therein the ideal worth and dignity of his unfallen condition, and even now, when only a broken fragment of the sceptre with which once he ruled the world remains in his hand, such he is commanded to regard himself still."

fectly consistent, nay, inevitably demanded, provided the earth is unique; but it is altogether incompatible with the scientific view which regards this as a paltry world in the midst of immeasurable other worlds of the same sort, and of vastly grander proportions. It is a pertinent question, which will never fail of being asked, How is it possible that the Divine One could consistently leave the glories of his empire to dwell upon a mote — a mote so small that its absence, with that of all its inhabitants, would scarcely be missed from the physical universe?

We are aware that to these questions various explanations have been given. This, that, and the other relief from the difficulty have been beautifully, forcibly, and eloquently presented by Dr. Chalmers, whom no writer has surpassed in these discussions; but still, after the exhilaration of his sentences is exhausted, we inevitably feel ourselves falling back into the train of customary thought and ordinary expression; and the reaction, in spite of ourselves, arouses suspicions adverse to revelation. In point of fact, a reconciliation between the theological and scientific view is reached, if reached at all, through unnatural distortions. We weep and fear; the conviction stares us full in the face that the fundamental idea of Christianity is, that every man, of the lowest cast, and outcast even, is of more value than all the physical worlds flying in majesty and grandeur above us, together with everything they contain; and also, that intensity of interest throughout the spiritual universe is centred upon this earth, because it alone is the home of a class of beings the like of which nowhere else exists — beings who are in the line of promotion to the highest positions bestowed upon any created intelligences. Whereas, on the other hand, as already pointed out, if all these regions of space are full of inhabitable and inhabited worlds, then this little earth on which we dwell, with all its inhabitants, is, as Whewell forcibly expresses it, "*annihilated* by the magnitudes about us." *

In the present review of the general question before us we are not to ask, what *can* God do, but what *has* he done, and what are the facts which can be deduced in support of given speculations. This limitation will, we think, not only be allowed, but demanded, by every intelligent reader; for otherwise there would be no limit to the possibilities that may be imposed upon us by fertile imaginations. We may imagine civilized and religious inhabitants upon the diminutive planetoids, upon meteoric stones, and upon the wild and bare volcanic peaks of the moon; we may suppose that the entire celestial ether is inhabited by responsible beings; we may say, if disposed, that there are a million intelligences like ourselves holding wise converse upon the rich tapestry of a sunset-cloud; we may assert, with Giordano and Bruno, that the interior of the earth is inhabited; that the fabled Ariel and sylphs people the air, that naiads and water-sprites people the seas, that gnomes inhabit the darkness, and salamanders the fire. But clearly enough all such imaginary suppositions are to be ruled out of the present discussion. To make clear our position in a word, it is this: inasmuch as science proves that the astro-

* Appendix B.

nomical bodies are uninhabitable by physical and moral agents something like ourselves, by exactly so much may our confidence be re-established in the direct biblical representations, but shaken respecting a plurality of inhabited worlds.

It hardly need be stated that facts bearing upon these matters are at present numerous and reliable to an extent hardly dreamed of until of late. The physical sciences are now systematized as never before, and within the past few years have been making almost incredible advances. Political economy has so arranged avocations in harmony with the principles of division of labor, that every man is allowed and asked to give exclusive attention to his favorite field of investigation. The astronomer may study the heavens, while the manufacturer clothes him, and the agriculturist feeds him, and the merchant holds for exchange his products and needed supplies, while the mechanic builds his observatory, the machinist manufactures his wonderful instruments of observation, and while the mathematician furnishes his no less wonderful tables of calculation; and each in turn receives an almanac in compensation thereof. With such facilities at hand, with all the modern improvements of art and invention, it would be marvellous if there were not occasion to change some of the hypotheses that were started years ago by such men as Copernicus, Galileo, and Kepler, and ably defended by Chalmers and his followers.

It is also too well known hardly to allow mention, that the physical condition of the heavenly bodies was formerly ascertained solely by means of astronomical and mathematical calculations. Their weight, distances, and relative density were estimated, very early, with surprising approximation. But more recently, estimates have been reduced to a nicety and precision almost incredible. The science of chemistry, as well as the higher mathematics, has come to the aid of those engaged upon these matters. The chemist and the astronomer have harmoniously joined their forces. An astronomical observatory has now appended to it a stock of appliances such as hitherto was only to be found in the chemical laboratory. A devoted corps of volunteers of all nations have directed their telescopic and spectroscopic artillery to every region of the universe. The sun, the spots on his surface, the corona, and the red and yellow prominences seen round him during total eclipses, the moon, the planets, comets, auroras, nebulæ, white stars, yellow stars, red stars, variable and temporary stars, each tested by the prism, is compelled to show its distinguishing prismatic colors. Rarely before in the history of science has enthusiastic perseverance, directed by penetrative genius, produced within ten years so brilliant a succession of discoveries. It is not merely the chemistry of sun and stars that is subjected to analysis by the spectroscope; the laws of their being are now subjects of direct investigation; and already we have glimpses of their evolutional history through the stupendous power of this most subtile and delicate test: thus solar and stellar chemistry have been succeeded by solar and stellar physiology.*

* Sir William Thomson.

So admirably is this work done, that the light from every visible orb that hangs in or flashes over the sky, even the most distant, is taken into the laboratory, is analyzed, and sifted, and made to report as to what is the physical and chemical construction and composition of those orbs: their relative weight is also thereby estimated, and their moments measured with approximate accuracy; spectrum analysis may yet correct the most exact mathematical calculations hitherto received.* This union of optics, math-

* The science of spectrum analysis has so far modified the whole system of astronomy that we may state in a word the principles upon which it is applied. It is ascertained upon experiment that any solid, liquid, or gas, when heated until luminous, gives off a light peculiar to itself. Upon the spectrum each peculiar light finds its exact place, and shows its peculiar characteristics, by means of the lines it assumes thereon; so that by the spectra of any light known, be it moon-light, planet-light, sun-light, gas-light, or the light from any other substance, its chemical character can be accurately detected. One can also, thereby, trace resemblances and dissimilarities between our earth and the other heavenly bodies, and thus ascertain, at once, whether or not they are inhabitable. This science of spectrum analysis, it should be noticed, is not recent in all its particulars. It has had an historic growth.

The prismatic analysis of light was first discovered by Newton, and was estimated by himself as being "the oddest, if not the most considerable, detection which hath hitherto been made in the operations of nature." But the obtaining of a pure spectrum, with the discovery of the dark lines, was reserved for the nineteenth century. Our fundamental knowledge of the dark lines is due solely to Fraunhofer. Wollaston saw them, but did not discover them. Brewster labored long and well to perfect the prismatic analysis of

ematics, and chemistry has relieved the science of modern astronomy of many of its former uncertainties, and has thrown over it an imposing splendor that renders it one of the most inspiring and ennobling, as well as attractive fields of investigation. Astronomical science is no longer in its cradle, but has shown its face in public, and left off its childish prattle. "Formerly one man observed the stars for all Christendom, and the rest of the world observed *him*. But now, up and down Europe and North America, from the deep blue of Italian skies to the cold, frosty atmospheres of St. Petersburg and Glasgow, from the clear sky of New England to the salubrious atmosphere of California, the stars are conscious of being

sun-light; he laid important foundations for a grand superstructure, which he scarcely lived to see. Piazzi Smyth, by spectroscopic observation performed on the Peak of Teneriffe, added greatly to our knowledge of the dark lines produced in the solar spectrum by the absorption of our own atmosphere. The prism became an instrument for chemical qualitative analysis in the hands of Fox Talbot and Herschel. But the application of this test to solar and stellar chemistry had never been suggested, either directly or indirectly, by any other naturalist, when Stokes taught it in Cambridge, at some time prior to the summer of 1852.

To the toil of Kirchhoff and of Angstrom we owe large-scale maps of the solar spectrum. These maps now constitute the standards of reference for all workers in the field. Plucker and Hittorf made the important discovery of changes in the spectra of ignited gases produced by changes in the physical condition of the gas. Lockyer and Fälkland have furnished us with the effects of varied pressure upon the quality of light emitted by glowing gases.

everywhere watched, and can no longer hide from us their mysteries." *

Seventy years ago Dr. Chalmers conjectured that the time might come when astronomical instruments would arrive at such perfection as to afford an observer an inside view of the planets. He had no misgiving, apparently, should that time arrive, that we would see men like ourselves, "with as close resemblance," — to employ an expression of some early astronomer, — "as that existing between one egg and another." But these rapid advances, by means of new appliances, which have brought under our range new and hitherto unexplained phenomena, report less and less in favor of the scientific, but more and more in support of the theological idea; so much so that no well-informed person will now venture to repeat the assertions of former writers as to the general inhabitableness of the physical universe.†

Comets and Zodiacal Lights.‡ — Who has seen

* De Quincey.

† Perhaps our spiritualistic friends desire us to make an exception in case of a so-well-informed person as Mr. Andrew Jackson Davis. He seems to have more than realized, it is true, the most sanguine expectations of the great Scotch divine; for he has seen with the naked eye (if we believe his claims) all those things which Dr. Chalmers desired to see but could not, or, if possible, more incredible still, he has visited our planetary neighbors in person, and has made their intimate acquaintance. A spiritualistic friend told us the other day that science could never go beyond spiritual clairvoyance, and that, therefore, all views at variance with those of Mr. Davis should be abandoned.

‡ Of zodiacal light we shall say not much, since so little is

one of those bodies which we call comets, which at times spreads out its silvery veil over a third part of the visible heavens, without being filled with delight or wonder? How startling the journeys of these bodies! From cold, ice-bound regions beyond the planetary system they come, onward towards the sun they go, into its very face and eyes they fly, until he glares upon them with twenty-five thousand six hundred times fiercer heat than that with which a vertical sun at midday scorches our equator, and then away they return to another baptism in regions of eternal frost.

The matter of which comets are composed was long since known to be of the least appreciable specific gravity. The comet of 1847, known as Miss Mitchel's, passed directly over a star of the fifth magnitude; and yet its light, which would have been entirely obliterated by a moderate fog extending only a few yards from the earth, appeared in no way enfeebled. "I have examined," says General Mitchel, "the most minute telescopic stars, and have received their light undimmed, though it had penetrated thousands and tens of thousands of miles of this cometary matter." The evidence is conclusive that the comet is only vapor, and almost perfectly transparent. The most fleecy and gossamer clouds that rest in the sky, or are driven hither and thither by the idlest breath of a fitful summer breeze, is a hundred fold more sub-

really known respecting it. It is, doubtless, a solar appendage, perhaps of the nature of comets, or of meteors. Certainly, judging from the present reports of scientific investigation, it is something not very distinct from one or the other.

stantial than the comet. It is claimed by those who have carefully investigated these subjects, that the substance of comets is so attenuated that if their diameter were a hundred thousand miles, having a proportionate length, they would not contain so much matter as would be required to fill an ordinary-sized gentleman's hat. The convulsions feared should a comet some time strike the earth are altogether beyond the possibility of taking place. These phosphorescent, rather fluorescent, bodies are found to be composed largely of pure vapor of carbon.*

Here, then, are certain bodies of vast proportions, the largest objects in the solar system, of magnificent appearance, self-luminous, and also to a certain extent reflective, which are of such a character as to so far preclude the idea of inhabitants that not an intelligent and informed advocate of such an idea can, first or last, be found. Now, may we not apply the same reasoning to comets which is applied to other astronomical bodies? Have we not a right to ask, Why were comets created, unless they are inhabited? Why did God make these grand displays of physical phenomena, sending them flying through the universe in exact orbits and with exact periods, unless they somehow bear upon their vapory and gas-lit surface intelligent and moral beings? How can an astro-

* The light of Brorsen's comet has been subjected to critical spectrum analysis, and found to be nearly identical with that of highly heated vapor of carbon. The composition of this comet (and it is doubtless true of all others), by chemical analysis, discloses also an ingredient which does not coincide with anything now known upon the earth.

nomical body be so charming, grand, and vast in its proportions if it is not peopled with intelligences? And if not thus peopled, is it not evidence that there is a glaring inconsistency between the divine wisdom, skill, and benevolence, on the one hand, and such a needless expenditure of creative energy on the other? Such are the facts: let each answer for himself.

Shooting Stars, Meteors, and Aërolites. — These names represent bodies of the same general physical character;* the difference between them is one of circumstance only. The shooting star disappears when far up the sky; the meteor comes near to us, but disappears, sometimes with loud reports, before reaching the earth, while the aërolite reaches the earth unconsumed. Some of these displays, especially the October and November meteoric showers, are grand and imposing, and numberless eyes watch them from nightfall until dawn-light. These bodies belong to systems which revolve about the sun with the regularity of planets. They are as independent in their creation as Jupiter or the sun; they are not mere fuel for the sun to feed upon, as certain astronomers have conjectured; they retard, rather than increase, his flames; they are not, as Figuier supposes, mere mes-

* Aërolites bring us, of known substances, oxide of iron, oxides of nickel, of cobalt, and of manganese, magnesia, lime, silica, copper, and sulphur, and have the appearance of having been changed to a solid from a liquid state under a dense atmosphere of hydrogen gas. Meteors are dissipated in their passage through the air, but the unconsumed part sometimes falls to the earth in the form of dust of yellow chloride of iron. Cometary meteors we need not discuss.

sengers sent to us across space from other worlds, to tell us of the composition of their soil; nor, as Sir William Thomson suggests, are they express trains from other worlds to ours, freighted with the germs of life and seeds of vegetation. These interesting visitants come rather, without reasonable doubt, from trains of small planets, little asteroids, which circle around the sun, forming different systems, and constituting belts analogous to Saturn's rings; and the reason for the comparatively large number of meteors which we observe annually about the 14th of November is, that at that time the earth's orbit cuts through some meteoric belt. We have probably not yet passed through the very nucleus, or densest part; but thirteen times, in Octobers and Novembers, from October 13, A. D. 902, to November 14, 1866, inclusive (this last time having been correctly predicted by Professor Newton, of Yale College), we have, by actual observation, passed through a part of the belt greatly denser than the average. When in their revolution these bodies encounter the earth's atmosphere, they are ignited by friction, and give us safe and inexpensive, but magnificent displays of fireworks. The aggregate number of the meteoric systems is beyond calculation, and the number of meteors composing each system is next to infinite.*

* Professor Newton calculates, upon reliable data, that, on an average, in the course of a single day 7,500,000 meteors, large enough to be visible to the naked eye, are consumed in the earth's atmosphere, and about 400,000,000 meteors, visible *through a telescope* of moderate power, are thus consumed. Fifty points of radiation, at least, have been already discovered.

Though knowing little of their extent and number, they tell us some things of importance. They report, as does everything else in the universe, how lavish is the Creator in his expenditures; not merely bread enough, but bread to spare, is the law of his kingdom — a fact which is loaded with analogies against the theory of a plurality of inhabited worlds.

The Nebulæ constitute a class of astronomical bodies concerning which there has been, perhaps, more discussion than respecting any others. These starry clusters, or patches of "starry powder," so called, seem to be of endless extent; they rise one above another, and appear without limit to stretch away into God's immensity. Two theories, radically differing from one another, cover the various speculations presented. The first and oldest supposes them to be stellar clusters. Such a conclusion is natural, for at first sight they appear to be stars seen through mist. Powerful telescopes have been able to resolve some of them into distinct points of light; suppositions were rife that with more powerful instruments of observation all the nebulous clusters could be thus resolved. It was further argued that each cluster constitutes a distinct stellar system. In harmony with this supposition, our sun is to be looked upon as an individual star, forming only a single unit in a cluster or mass of many millions of other similar stars, — a mere fragment in the midst of a universe of similar solar systems, represented as everywhere teeming with human inhabitants, subject to the same thoughts, experiences, and developments as characterize ourselves.

The second, known as the Laplace theory, regards the nebulæ as a luminous fluid, diffused through the universe, being now in a formative state, becoming, or soon to become, distinct stellar systems, like our own. It was natural for sceptical physicists, upon embracing this idea, to conclude that by natural processes, and without the intervention of a Creator, these nebulæ are to become distinct systems, then completed worlds, which in time have the inherent power of producing plants, and brutes, and man.

The first of these theories is now generally set aside. Among other things there has been of late a radical change as to the supposed distances of the nebulæ. Professor Roscoe informs us that the opinion that their remoteness is what makes it so difficult to resolve them can no longer be upheld, and that their nebulous appearance is not on account of their great distance, but because of the highly attenuated condition of the substances composing them.*

* It is also the opinion of Sir John Herschel, supported by Lord Rosse, that the nebulæ, as a class of objects, are not more distant than the nearest fixed stars. Said David Gill, in an address before the Edinburgh meeting of the British Association (1871), "From observations extending over eleven months, I concluded that the planetary nebula No. 37, in Herschel's 4th catalogue, possessed a very measurable parallax, and a considerable proper motion. Should further measures confirm this result, the true inference to be drawn is, that some of the planetary nebulæ, at least, are nearer to us than the fixed stars, and probably perform an entirely distinct part in the economy of nature." "There are vast numbers of the nebulæ," says Lord Rosse, "much too faint to be sketched or measured with any prospect of advantage, the

But in addition to the more accurate telescopic examinations we have also the report of spectrum analysis, which forever sets at rest the question of the physical character of the nebulæ. They can no longer, in the light of this science, to say the least, be represented as suns like ours. When Mr. Huggins brought the image of the nebulæ upon the slit of his spectroscope, he found that he no longer had to do with a class of *bodies* of the nature even of stars! *

most powerful instruments we possess showing in them nothing of an organized structure, but merely a confused mass of nebulosity of varying brightness." "I believe," says Proctor, "that future researches will prove, not only that the Milky Way, as a whole, is much nearer than we have been imagining, but that portions of it are absolutely nearer to us than the brightest of the single stars." The researches of Huggins, Secchi, and Wüllner, seem to indicate that the temperature of the nebulæ is extremely high; but those of Zollner, Frankland, and Lockyer indicate a comparatively low temperature. It is claimed by others that a moderate process of condensation would develop, from cool matter, as great an amount of heat as nebulous or stellar masses have as yet evinced.

* "The conclusion," says Roscoe, "is obvious, that the close association of points of light in a nebula can no longer be accepted as proof that the object consists of true stars. These luminous points, in some nebulæ at least, must be regarded as portions of matter denser, probably, than the outlying parts of the great nebulous mass, but still gaseous."

The same writer, in another connection, affirms "that the nebulæ are not groups of far-distant suns, because we find that the light which some of them give out is not the kind of light which such far-distant fixed stars must emit." Sir William Thomson, indorsing the discoveries of Huggins, claims that the light of the nebulæ, so far as hitherto sensi-

The light of some of them is very feeble. Mr. Lockyer estimates that an ordinary sperm candle a quarter of a mile distant, would give off a light twenty thousand times more brilliant. Two thirds of the nebulæ thus far examined are unhesitatingly pronounced gaseous. They are composed of nitrogen and hydrogen united with certain unknown elements. It has been doubted by high authority whether a single nebula can be pointed out which contains light enough "to light a good-sized room." In view of all these facts, we seem forced to the conclusion that these numberless masses and points of light, which were formerly supposed to be suns like the sun in our planetary system, and which were thought to be attended by inhabited planets countless in number, are for the most part luminous gas; those that are irresolvable are, at most, but primitive "fire-mist" "light;" while the resolvable are still in a gaseous state, though farther advanced than the irresolvable. We are misled by the term frequently employed — "clouds of fiery dust" — even, for, as a class of objects, the nebulæ, like the comets, many of them, — two thirds at least, — are nothing but heated vapor. Respecting the remaining one third, it is shown that as compared with

ble to us, proceeds from incandescent hydrogen and nitrogen gases. Mr. Tait suggests that they may be gaseous exhalations, ignited by collisions between meteoric stones.

"The spectroscope shows us," says David Gill, "that these nebulæ are not stars, but incandescent gas. I am reported as saying that the conclusion I had arrived at was, that the nebula '*was not a collection of matter, but a fixed star.*' This is entirely wrong, and would have been more nearly correct had it been reversed."

our solar system they are not at all complete; they are spiral in their movements and confused in their masses; their forms are irregular, and destitute of any apparent system; there seems not the slightest evidence that they have passed from their original chaotic state. To insist upon covering them, or any of their dependencies, with living intelligence, is, in the light of modern scientific inquiry, the wildest conjecture possible. If the theory of Laplace is true, they are certainly uninhabitable; while the earlier and opposite theory, as we have seen, has at present not the slightest foundation.*

One might as well live in the zodiacal light, or upon the intangible twilight, or upon the northern aurora, or in a gas flame, as upon the nebulæ. There is as much evidence that those vast cumulous clouds of midsummer, which assume all kinds of fantastic shapes, — alpine mountains and royal palaces, — tinged with the richest tints of sunrise and sunset, are the abodes of life, as to suppose that these almost-interminable tracts of nebulous matter are inhabited.

To emphasize this thought is unnecessary, other than at the single point of its bearing upon the argument from analogy and the consistency of things. All that has been said clearly weakens the force of these arguments. If we mistake not, they begin to menace

* While the theory of Laplace, as a whole, has been of late years growing in favor, and justly so, still it must be confessed that it is beset, at certain points, with many objections. The nebulæ are resolvable by the telescope, from a supposed mass of fluid, into distinct elements, and by the spectroscope from a solid or liquid state into the most attenuated gas.

those who have hitherto employed them; at least, the advocates of a plurality of inhabited worlds find, yearly, less and less encouragement in the varied results of scientific investigation. Nineteen twentieths of the beautiful objects which glimmer in the midnight heavens, and which a few years since were thought by some to be inhabitable, are now transferred, without a dissenting voice, from the scientific to the theological side of this question. Man need no longer be abashed, regarding himself a mere mote, but may smile and lift his hand for the crown and sceptre which revelation has so manifestly designated as his exclusive possession.

Fixed Stars are those self-luminous and twinkling orbs which occupy regions beyond our solar system, and which in stellar space rise, many deep, to heights and distances incomprehensible. Advocates of "more worlds than one" have been very confident and jubilant over data from this source. From the magnitude of these bodies and their resemblance to our sun, they have been claimed, with confidence which scarcely listens to objection, to be centres of systems of inhabited worlds in no respects inferior to the planets of our solar system, and in many respects vastly superior. Before we can feel at liberty, however, to admit all that has been presented for our unqualified acceptance respecting the fixed stars, we certainly have the right to enter upon a re-examination of former suppositions in the light of facts which modern scientific investigation presents to us.

As early as 1814, Fraunhofer discovered that the spectra of the various fixed stars which he examined differ from that of the sun and planets. He came, thus early, to the remarkable conclusion that the chemical constitution of the fixed stars must therefore, in some respects, differ from that of our solar system. There are differences so great between the fixed stars themselves, however, that such a sweeping conclusion as this of Fraunhofer may not be admitted by every one, especially by those who find certain strong analogies between our sun and some of the fixed stars.

A more recent statement is that of Professor Roscoe, which will doubtless be regarded by many as authoritative. "We have now arrived," he says, "at a distinct understanding of the physical constitution of the fixed stars: they consist of a white-hot nucleus, giving off a continuous spectrum, surrounded by an incandescent atmosphere, in which exist the absorbent vapors of the particular metals." But with this general statement we can hardly rest satisfied, since the different classes of fixed stars report to us, in each case, data distinct and characteristic.

Stars of Variable Lustre form a curious class, and are at present studied with special interest. From our distant point of view they appear remarkably beautiful. But when the telescope and spectroscope, aided by the imagination, enable us to stand within hailing distance, nay, to plant our feet upon their surface and to penetrate beneath their fiery exterior, we find that the sublime energies which are at work upon and within them are well nigh appalling; settled at once is the question of their inhabitability, and that of any system of planets which may or may not be revolving about them. The variableness, so beautiful to the naked eye, but so terrible to the eye of science, is the result of enormous and sometimes sudden explosions of hydrogen gas. This fierce augmentation of light and heat would terminate the supposed organized planetary life in an instant.* No less fearful for these conjectured planetary inhabitants is the sudden diminution, and in some instances the entire extinction, of the light of the variable stars. Think of a system of inhabited worlds having a sun brilliant as ours, which perceptibly begins to wane with no returning spring-time! † Or think of a system of worlds flooded one day with light and heat, the next plunged into the thickest darkness, and locked in the embrace of universal ice! Sorrowful, indeed, the plight of those inhabitants.‡

* Professor Roscoe bears out Lockyer and Jannsen in a calculation that if the intensity of the sun's rays were increased no more than were those of the stars in the Northern Crown in May, 1866, our solid globe would be dissipated in vapor almost as soon as a drop of water in a furnace. The temperature in the sunlight would rise at once to that only attainable in the focus of the largest burning-glass.

† The first two stars in Hydra, in less than a human lifetime, changed, in the seventeenth century, from the fourth to the eighth magnitude, so that the most fearful and perpetual winter succeeded what had been perpetual summer. A notable star in the Swan varies from the fifth to the tenth magnitude. A star in Cepheus changes in five days from the third to the fifth magnitude. A star in Lyra in six days diminishes from the third to the fifth magnitude. A star in the Whale is subjected to remarkable changes; waxing, waning, disappearing, and then relighting its flames, and shining for a time with steady brilliancy.

‡ A noted star in the Great Bear vanished in the eighteenth century; the eighth and ninth stars of Taurus have also disappeared; the fifty-fifth star of Hercules, a star in Auriga, the eleventh in Lupus, and several others in the catalogue of

Nay, these appearances may indicate that the entire class of variable and periodic stars are self-luminous bodies, as yet destitute of permanent forms, and likewise destitute of attending regular planetary systems.

Another class of fixed stars, known as *double* or *compound stars*, possess certain remarkable features. The earlier term, " double," is hardly exact, for many are found to be not only double, but triple, quadruple, and even multiple. M. Struve is authority for saying that not less than one in three or four of the fixed stars are compound. Still more remarkable is the fact that different parts of compound stars often shine with different colors. A combination frequently occurring is crimson and blue.* The singular vicissitudes of light diffused upon the attendant planets (if they are attended), in consequence of two suns in their firmament, is well nigh inconceivable by the poor mortals inhabiting the earth, who have but a single sun to light the day and a single moon to reflect the sun-light by night. In general, such suns will rise at different times. When the blue sun rises, it will for a time preside alone in the heavens, diffusing a blue morning. Its crimson companion, however, soon appearing, the lights of both being blended in the strongest combination at intervals, may result in a midday of white light. As evening approaches, and the two orbs descend towards the western horizon, the blue sun will first set,

Ptolemy, have vanished, leaving their planetary inhabitants to raise their crops and grope their way under star-light.

* The combination red and green is found in Hercules and Cassiopeia; brown and green, also brown and blue, in the Whale, Giraffe, Orion, Gemini, and Swan.

leaving the crimson one alone in the heavens, and like a mighty conflagration will light up the western sky, and close the day. As the year rolls on, these changes will be varied in every conceivable manner. At those seasons when the suns are on opposite sides of the planet, crimson and blue days will alternate, without any intervening night; and at the intermediate epochs all the various intervals of rising and setting of the two suns will be exhibited. Clouds, waters, and vegetation will each share in this multiplicity of changing hues.* The romance of all this witchery of star wonders is still further enhanced upon the discovery of stars which have the extraordinary power of changing their color, — rightly named "chameleon stars." One of the components of a double star in Hercules changed, in twelve years, from yellow, through gray, cherry red, and a most beautiful red, to yellow again. The variations produced, in consequence, cannot be described, nor realized, nor scarcely imagined.

But it should be ever borne in mind that the more wonderful these marvels of stellar condition, the more inevitably are all these stars removed from the field of analogy, and the more surely are they rendered uninhabitable. The spectrum of every colored star, as we are assured by Kirchhoff, wants certain rays existing in our solar spectrum. We find, therefore, as in case of the nebulæ, that those of the fixed stars which are variable and compound, though grand and imposing astronomical bodies, are very far from helping the cause of More Worlds than One. But it is asked, Are there not white stars which present strong and unques-

* Professor Lardner. Appendix C.

tioned analogies between themselves and the sun? It has been so claimed. Our knowledge of some of them is yet limited. While awaiting additional facts, we must bear in mind that nothing yet like a planet has been discovered revolving around any one of the fixed stars. The absence of regular motion among the fixed stars; the slowness of their changes, indicating extreme rarity; their gyratory movements, indicating crudeness, long since led Humboldt to maintain the opinion that the whole weight of analogy is against existing similarity between the sun and the fixed stars. The earlier supposition of Herschel, that some of the fixed stars — Alpha, Centauri, and Sirius — emit more light than the sun, is also now set aside as untenable. Later investigations, based upon a more accurate and extended observation of phenomena, show that their light in many instances is less than that of the sun, and that in this respect our sun, instead of being one of the least, is among the more important objects in the entire physical universe.

The hypothesis so grandly stated by General Mitchell and others, that the sun, with its retinue of planets, is revolving about some distant centre, in common with other solar systems, is very far from receiving general indorsement. Regularity of motion in the solar system can be explained more easily upon a less complicated hypothesis. The earlier speculations of Kant, Lambert, and Wright (middle of the eighteenth century), subsequently indorsed and confirmed by Sir W. Herschel, that the Milky Way is a projection on the sphere of a stratum of stars, in the midst of which our sun and system are placed, with a possible centre towards Sirius, is much more in harmony with recent discoveries.* Who can tell but ours is the only ripe sun in the universe! We may be forced to the conclusion, after all, that the grandest created thing is not at the large but at the small end of the telescope. It may turn out that a human being, with a telescope in one hand, a spectroscope in the other, and himself endowed with imagination, and not some actual inhabitant on those beautiful stars, is the one for whom magnificent stellar entertainments have been nightly given. The conceptions of Herschel and Laplace are no less grand that they are earthlings than if they had been denizens of Algol or Mira. Madness must indeed be in the brain of the astronomer who falls not often upon his knees. God is not shorn of his glory, nor have his purposes met defeat, though Brewster and Dr. Chalmers should chance to have been mistaken. We thank the one for his profound reasonings and thrilling suppositions, and the other for his sublime rhetorical flights; but no man is infallible. "A theory," as Voltaire has quaintly remarked, "is like a mouse, which may successfully pass nineteen holes, but is stopped at the twentieth."

We thank Science for the much she has disclosed. We await yet greater revelations. Perhaps she will tell us anon that the astronomical centre of the physical

* The illustration first proposed by Herschel is, that the universe of stars presents a form similar to that of two watch crystals, brought together so as to form a hollow double convex, and that the solar system is placed in or near the centre. Proctor, in his *Essays on Astronomy*, p. 331, has a diagram, given for another purpose, which may, however, prove a correct representation of the stellar universe.

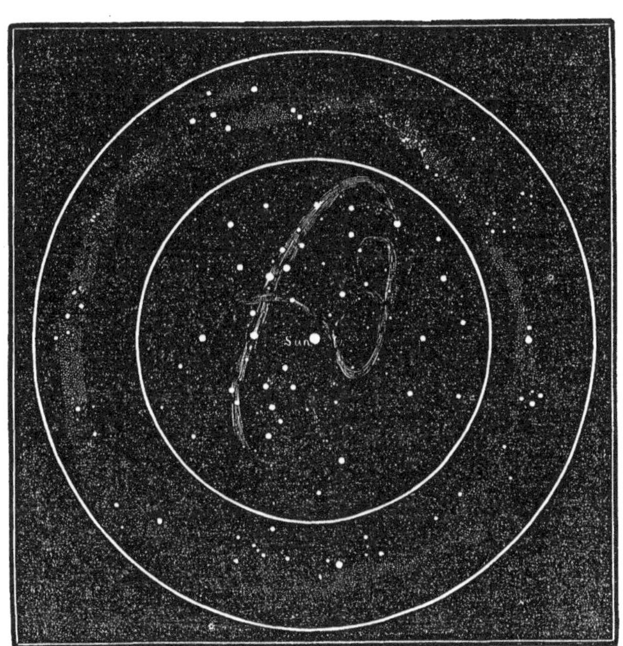

DIAGRAM FROM PROCTOR'S "ESSAYS ON ASTRONOMY."

universe is identical with its theological centre, — both being not far from the present home of humanity.

The Solar System. — The arguments from analogy and the consistency of things have been so weakened by investigations in the nebular and the stellar heavens that the theory of the general inhabitability of the solar system must be left to stand or fall upon its own merits; presumptions in favor of such views there are not.

The most majestic body in the solar system is the *Sun*. A theory, which gained for a time some headway, claims that beneath the phosphorescent atmosphere of the sun is a non-luminous atmosphere, surrounding an interior body protected from the exterior fiery rays, and thereby rendered suitable for habitation. "If," said Arago, "you ask me this question, Is the sun inhabited? I should answer that I know nothing about it. But if you ask me if the sun can be inhabited by beings organized like those who people our globe, I should not hesitate to answer, Yes."

This view is evidently an out-growth of the no longer tenable supposition that it is a wasteful economy to create grand and majestic bodies, and leave them destitute of intelligent inhabitants. Certainly, if such reasoning can anywhere apply, it is in the case before us. The size and magnificence of the sun resolutely demand inhabitants, if such characteristics furnish adequate reason for providing populations. To form a body equal to the sun in bulk, it would be necessary to roll into one nearly 1,400,000 globes of the size of our earth. Place together all the planets of our system, and as a product there would be a body five hundred times less in bulk than the sun. Therefore, according to the reasoning sometimes employed, if any spot in the solar system is inhabited, then, by all odds, must the sun be thronged with inhabitants. But we have already thrice seen that Science no longer listens to such arguments. No matter how great, no matter how grand, the object may be, — the telescope and spectroscope take it in hand to settle the question without leave or license, and without the least respect for our preconceptions. Aided by the telescope we look upon a conflagration in the sun of such immense and appalling proportions as would instantly destroy organized physical life, though distant from it by hundreds of thousands of miles. Under a July tropical sun, though ninety-four millions of miles away, we are full near enough for comfort. The theory of a non-luminous atmosphere is a tremendous and obstinate effort to render habitable a realm which is most manifestly uninhabitable.*

Lockyer, who has estimated the extent of the solar flames, has given us some startling figures. He has seen masses of flame leaping upward from the body of the sun twenty-seven thousand miles in height; and then, as if conscious of a defeated effort to destroy the universe, he has seen them settle back again to their ordinary level in a space of less than ten minutes.

* The heat at the sun's surface, by accurate experiment, is found to be prodigious. The fiercest blaze of a furnace gives off not a seventh part as much heat. What form of life is there which is adapted to such abodes? The test of polarization of light, applied by Arago, has conclusively shown that the luminous matter of the sun is gaseous. But perhaps men could be so conditioned as to live in gas-flame. (?)

Other flames have been seen to flash up to the enormous distance of from ninety to a hundred thousand miles. The vast volumes of smoke rising from these solar eruptions can be distinctly seen with the eye unaided by the telescope.* If any doubts have remained as to the accuracy of telescopic observations, they are now completely silenced by the science of spectrum analysis. There is at present no question but that the physical composition and exact chemical nature of the sun are accurately disclosed to us by the tests of the solar spectra under the experiments of such men as Bunsen and Kirchhoff.† They confirm observations made by telescopes, and the experiments of polarization, and fully restore the opinions of those philosophers of the middle ages who saw in the sun, not an inhabited world,—which, unless inhabited, would be a reproach to the wisdom of the Creator,—but a "globe of fire," a kind of "gigantic torch," which, together with the moon, was set "in the firmament of heaven, to give light upon the earth, and to rule over the day and over the night, and to divide the light from the darkness," expressly for the benefit of man.‡

* This is, doubtless, the most satisfactory explanation of the spots visible upon the sun's surface. The view that they are produced by the sudden fall upon the sun's surface of immense quantities of meteoric matter, which, by force of concussion, fusion, and ignition, are afterwards converted into solar-fuel, or that they are produced by terrific tornadoes, sweeping over the sun's surface, similar to those which sometimes visit our own tropics, are theories which can hardly be said to have, at the present time, the support of science. See Appendix D.

† Appendix E.

‡ Gen. i. 17–19.

The planets are to us the nearest visible astronomical bodies. They have known analogies between themselves and the earth more striking and more numerous than have any of the bodies already examined. Very confident have been many writers, that human inhabitants occupy the planets, who differ not much, if in any respect, from ourselves. Others, with equal confidence, have pointed out certain important differences distinguishing the various planetary inhabitants. But those who of late have given the subject anything like critical attention have concluded that the most which has heretofore been written respecting planetary inhabitants is purely visionary, and so arbitrary in its character as to preclude its reception as in the least degree reliable. Dr. Chalmers kept within the bounds of reasonable conjecture; but certain others — Sir Humphry Davy, Fontenelle, Christian Wolf, and Andrew Jackson Davis, for illustration, — have allowed their enthusiasms and imaginations to run into all sorts of wild vagaries and extravagances. The inhabitants of the planet Saturn are represented by Davy as effecting their locomotion by the agency of six wings. Their arms, he says, resemble the trunks of elephants; and though in form they are a species of zoöphyte, still they are more intelligent than man.

Fontenelle likewise favors us with the peculiar characteristics of the different planetary inhabitants. Some he represents as exceedingly phlegmatic, others lively and agile as the most active Frenchman. Some are like the Moors of Granada, and still others like fur-clad Laplanders.

The inhabitants of Mercury are represented by Huygens as pre-eminently scientific, their close proximity to the sun giving them peculiar advantages in astronomical investigations. Christian Wolf, the German astronomer, estimates that the inhabitants of Jupiter are fourteen feet in height by eye measurement. But Proctor, by a course of reasoning equally clear, shows that they are but two and a half feet in height.* Andrew Jackson Davis stands in advance of all others in furnishing definite information upon this subject. Of course his announcements must be received as reliable, (?) for he is claimed by modern medium spiritualists, as already remarked, to be the most wonderful clairvoyant medium of the age, and is supposed to have visited in person the various planets he has so minutely described, and to have held consultation in person with these our planetary kindred.

There are, according to this distinguished oracle, two classes of inhabitants upon the planet Saturn. Those of the first and lower class are represented as very muscular; their bodies are rather wide than otherwise, and not perfectly round; they have great strength and elasticity of movement; they have more extensive scope of mental comprehension than the inhabitants of earth; and they are characterized by strong passions and love of mirth. On the other hand, the higher men of Saturn are represented as the perfection of physical development; their lungs, heart, and head, which are fully described by Mr. Davis, are the embodiment of health and perfection; their judgment is

* Appendix F.

so excellent (though we fail to see the connection) that they do not know what weakness or sickness means; the most difficult subjects are comprehended by one grasp of their gigantic intellects; they have telescopic eyes, which can reach through the entire solar system; they dwell in immense buildings, and live under a general free-love system similar to that advocated by Mr. Theodore Tilton.

The inhabitants of Jupiter are also, in substance, thus described by Mr. Davis: They are not in any respect fully up to the standard of those of Saturn; through a constitutional modesty they assume an inclined position closely resembling the modern Grecian bend; they are more highly intellectual and amiable than the inhabitants of earth; they are able to converse by the dexterous working or winking of the upper lip; their communities are made up of spiritual affinities, as in Saturn: in consequence, they multiply rapidly, and enjoy perfect health; they never die, but their bodies are changed by a process of felicitous evaporation; so enormous are their expansive and sweeping intellects that they comprehend all things and relations by a single concentrated thought; they live in tents upon the equator, and their society is an harmonious and happy brotherhood of medium spiritualists.

According to Mr. Davis, the peculiarity of the inhabitants of Mars is, that they have upon the tops of their heads no hair, resulting, it is possible, from the bondage in which for a long time they may have been held.

The inhabitants of Venus are noted for having a splendid breathing and digestive apparatus, the latter of which is quite necessary, as they eat with perfect impunity their own offspring.

The human inhabitants of Mercury are celebrated for their incessant activity, prodigious memories, and orang-outang appearance; they have no use for their ears, and fight with slings and stones. They have, as we should expect of such barbarians, no spiritualists among them, but are governed by an ignorant and self-constituted arbitration, and their church polity is probably Old School Presbyterian.

Favored as we are with so many and such definite accounts as to our outside kindred, it seems ungrateful not to accept these statements as final, especially since the rest of the stellar universe seems so ill suited for the purposes of habitation. Why not without controversy concede the point that the planets are each inhabited? Has not enough already been shown respecting the nebulæ and fixed stars to satisfy the theological argument? Shall we not be lonesome and homesick if there be no one beyond to hail and return our signals anon, when our sciences reach greater perfection? Possibly. A few additional facts, however, can injure no one; facts are dangerous only to the false.

Of the planets Uranus and Neptune, the arctic worlds, we say nothing, for their position places them beyond controversy; they are dark and vaporous worlds, frozen too, unless their internal and primeval fires are still smouldering.

The planet *Saturn* can, however, hardly be thus quickly passed by in silenec. It is a stupendous globe as compared with the earth; its volume is nearly nine hundred times greater; it is less imposing in its dimensions than Jupiter, but more magnificent in its surroundings. Eight moons sail through its heavens, presenting the varying phases of waxing and waning in striking contrasts and combinations; three rings, one nearly transparent, each having regular periodic revolutions, encircle this planet with their beautiful drapery. A lunar or solar eclipse upon our earth is a rare occurrence, and rivets the attention and interest of humanity. But upon Saturn the phenomenon is of daily occurrence. In some of its latitudes there may be seen one, two, three, and even four solar eclipses daily. Aside from these, there is every conceivable variety of eclipse coming from interpositions and conjunctions of sun, moons, and rings, resulting in a display of astronomical wonders which would thrill an intelligent eye-witness with inexpressible delight. Owing to these splendid arrangements and adornings of Saturn, it has been selected by advocates of more worlds than one as the abode of the most favored, intelligent, and exalted species of human creatures. But however remorseless it may seem to disturb and dislodge these imaginary inhabitants, modern science has presented certain facts, we are compelled to confess, before which past speculations vanish as the mists of morning. The density of this ringed world is now estimated to be no greater than that of the lightest cork. The sun appears to one upon its surface little else than a distant star. The rings, so beautiful to us under telescopic observation, produce an eclipse upon some parts of its surface of fifteen years' duration. The various phenomena which this planet presents to us were accounted for, until quite recently, upon the supposition that it has a nucleus of cinders at the centre surrounded by a vast extent of vapors scarcely more ponderous than a London fog; hence, if this is the correct supposition, men can no more inhabit Saturn than they can live in a mass of frozen mist, which the sun is never able to penetrate. The supposition now generally approved is, that Saturn consists of an unsolidified mass of star-stuff in process of cooling, subject to internal throes so tremendous as to upheave hundreds of square miles of its surface far above the ordinary level, giving it its frequent "square-shouldered" appearance. If this is the condition of Saturn, then, instead of frozen fog, the surrounding element is a mass of heated vapors and clouds which are continually rising from the seething fires beneath. This planet, according to this supposition, is as uninhabitable as a volcano, whose fires have subsided, but are far from extinguished.

The grandest exterior planet known to our system is *Jupiter*. Though at a distance which almost confounds the imagination, it is, when in the meridian, upon a winter's midnight, one of the most magnificent of the heavenly bodies. Roll together into one fourteen hundred worlds like our own, and there would result a planet no larger in bulk than Jupiter. Its stupendous magnitude with difficulty dawns upon us even under telescopic observation. When Galileo directed the first telescope to the examination of Jupiter, he discovered four minute objects which he at first supposed to be stars, but subsequently discovered to be moons like our own. The one nearest Jupiter, in the brief space of forty-two hours, goes through all its phases, from the thin, extended ring to the full and rounded circle. The progress of its changes is so rapid that it would be actually visible to a near eye-witness. The other satellites have longer periods, and are so arranged that one standing upon Jupiter would enjoy four different months at the same time, being in duration four, eight, seventeen, and forty days respectively. One would scarcely need a time-piece upon this planet, for its wonderful celestial clock-work is provided with its month, day, hour, minute, and even second hand. Littrow * highly congratulates the astronomers of Jupiter, inasmuch as the sunlight is so faint that, with the naked eye, they can see the stars at midday.

But there is another side to this enchanting picture. Littrow does not tell us whether agriculturists would be satisfied with the system of things found upon this planet; it would seem that while the astronomer was laughing everybody else would be found weeping.

Jupiter, at its greatest distance, is five hundred and eighteen millions of miles from the sun; the light and heat are therefore four fifths less than upon the earth; its days and nights will scarcely average five hours in length; its reflective power, as great as that of white paper, which renders the star so beautiful to us, is in consequence of perpetual banks of clouds and vapors, which Mädler, after careful examination, concludes must shut out from its surface, except from very narrow limits, all light from the sun. Even did the unobstructed sun-light fall directly upon the surface of this planet, only four tenths of the light thus received,

* Picture of the Heavens.

owing to the planet's reflective power, would be available for the purposes of economy. The former supposition of science, that Jupiter is a mass of ice-logged waters and frozen fogs surrounding central cinders of matter, answered the condition of most of the phenomena presented; but more recent investigations incline to the conclusion that this giant among the planets is a mass of fire-fluid bubbling and seething, but in such condition, however, as to emit for us but the slightest degree of light and heat. One or the other of the above suppositions is unquestionably true: in the one case the inhabitants of Jupiter must be aquatic men made up of frozen pulp; in the other case they must be such men as can live in a world whose entire surface is covered with vortices of active volcanoes, and whose atmosphere is gaseous exhalations equalled only by those of some pit infernal.*

From Jupiter we, for the present, pass by the Planetoids and Mars, the Earth, and the Moon, calling attention first to those planets which lie between us and the sun.

Mercury need not long detain us, since the most

* The eruptive action is especially observed upon Jupiter when it is nearest the sun; and likewise the sun's eruptive action is at that time the greatest, through their mutual attraction. The belts of Jupiter are, doubtless, due to the violent discharge of vapors from regions below its visible surface. Proctor concludes that Jupiter cannot be inhabited, but claims that its moons are favored with inhabitants. Perhaps we ought not to press one who is driven to such shifts; but the fact is, Jupiter's moons are as uninhabitable as would be our earth if scarcely a ray of illumination reached us from the sun.

frantic suppositions and imaginary contrivances have failed to render it inhabitable. A dense atmosphere has been proposed by some, a rare atmosphere by others, and a single and double envelope of clouds by certain others, as a means of modifying the intense heat of the sun's rays; but either supposition defeats the object sought, and proves about equally fatal to the imaginary inhabitants of this planet.* In fine, its close proximity to the sun giving it, when nearest the sun, ten times the light and heat we receive; its extreme density and general astronomical appearance indicating its utter destitution of water and atmosphere; its abrupt and extreme climatic changes, in consequence of its prodigious inclination (70°), —are conditions which,

* The ingenuity of some unscientific men, in these matters, is often very remarkable and amusing. For instance, when it was thought that the day of Venus was considerably longer than ours, it was clearly shown that such an arrangement is indispensable to this planet; but the day is found to be actually a little less than ours (23 hours, 21 minutes, 24 seconds). Likewise elaborate articles have appeared, showing how excellent is the arrangement of the rings and moons of Saturn and the moons of Jupiter, in order to give the extra and necessary light to these distant planets; but the fact is, that the multiple moon-light of Jupiter and Saturn is not a twentieth of that which our moon gives to the earth. Thus, likewise, in the case of Mercury; if the atmosphere is extremely dense, it would render the heat by day sufficient to boil water at the equator; if extremely rare, it would render the cold by night sufficient to congeal the gases, even; while an envelope of clouds sufficient to afford protection would, in the first place, require a dense atmosphere to support them, and, in the second place, would require a thickness of clouds such as to leave the planet in almost total darkness.

so far as we can imagine, render both animal and vegetable life impossible upon its surface.

The beautiful and conspicuous planet *Venus*, our morning and evening star, next greets us, but its reports, under scientific examination, vary not much from those of Mercury. The sun, as seen from its surface, would present magnificent but terrible phenomena. The inclination of the axis of Venus is such that there is poured down upon the same latitude an intensity of light and heat unknown at our equator in midsummer; but a little later there follows a polar winter, whose cold is such as to defy any known chemical test.* No flora or fauna known to the earth could endure for a single season such abrupt changes. Nor could the denizens of the arctic and sub-arctic regions live through the heat of a single midsummer's nightless day. Modifications of atmosphere such as to counteract these violent changes, would involve changes, as in case of Mercury, so great as to kill while they cure. Indeed, if Venus has any atmosphere, it must, owing to its extreme variations of temperature, be the home of incessant and furious tempests. The opinion is better established than any other, that Venus is destitute of water, and destitute of atmosphere, and that its surface differs not much from the crude slag which is cast out from glass manufactories.

The *Moon* brings us comparatively near home; it is

* "This planet has no temperate zone. The torrid and icy zones encroach the one upon the other, and rule successively over the regions which in our world constitute the temperate zone." M. BABINET.

only thirty diameters of the earth distant; we could reach it, travelling at ordinary railroad speed, in a half year. Professor Phillips, before the British Association, stated that spots only a few hundred feet in area could be easily detected. A crop of wheat removed from a field, or, as Herschel states, the construction or the devastation of a fair-sized city, would be quickly noticed by our astronomers. Yet never a change has been observed upon its surface. One of its hemispheres is forever hidden from the earth, the other is continually looking down upon it. Its unchangeable features tell us that never a cloud hangs in the lunar sky, while the absence of all refraction after the occultation of star-light, renders it absolutely certain that the moon is entirely destitute of anything that can be called an atmosphere. It appears to be in the same advanced stage, and is probably identical in substance, with aerolites.* Its geological history has all the interest of a romance. It was once "fire-mist," or "sun-stuff," "star-stuff," or "world-stuff," as variously named, which is probably the original created substance, "light" — God said, Let there be light (sun-stuff), and light (sun-stuff) was. Later the moon witnessed activities like those now at work in the sun. It was at that time a world on fire, whose flames reached far towards the earth; later the flames subsided, and, like Jupiter at the present time, the moon became a

* Should the moon fall towards the earth, it would upon striking our atmosphere be ignited by friction. If consumed before reaching the earth's surface, it would be a shooting star; if it reached comparatively near us, it would be a meteor; if it reached the earth's surface, it would be an aerolite.

bubbling mass of fire, having but slight illumination; at this stage an atmosphere appeared containing moisture; * this moisture, condensing and falling upon the surface, would be thrown off in the form of steam and vapor; subsequently, as the cooling process went on, waters remained upon the surface, rivers flowed from the mountains and emptied themselves into the lunar seas. In the course of time the moisture penetrated deeper and deeper, the internal fires were entirely quenched, the thirsty rocks drank up every drop of water, and then, as if insatiable, absorbed the very atmosphere, leaving the moon as we now find it, a home of desolation, an "abandoned camp," a "fossil world," an "ancient cinder," a mass of rough slag,† whose reflecting power does not much differ from that of a gray, weathered, sandstone rock. No atmosphere! ‡ No water! Beautiful in all its phases, hung in the heavens to preach to man of the fate now impending over the earth unless an infinite Providence shall cut short the days of desolation by a merciful and prophesied catastrophe.§

* It is estimated that one eighth of the glowing hydrogen composing the flames of the sun is convertible into pure water.

† Phillips.

‡ Zollner, Bond, and Herschel.

§ See 2 Pet. iii. 10–14. It is estimated at the present time, owing to the internal fires of the earth, that water and air are able to penetrate less than one fiftieth of the distance to the earth's centre; therefore, long before these fires are extinguished, the terrestrial water and atmosphere, like those of the moon, will have disappeared from the surface of a worn-out world. But for some providential interference the fate, not only of the earth, but of all celestial bodies, is written upon the face of the moon; the sun itself will become a lump of frozen matter, darkening the heavens.

We now return to *Mars*, the planet which, for special reasons, was reserved to complete our list.* It has been called the miniature earth. "It is the only object in the heavens which is known to exhibit features resembling those of our earth." † Its density, the length of its days, its seasons and years, are not widely different from those of the earth. The inhabitants of this planet (if it is inhabited) would have some advantages and some disadvantages as compared with the earth's inhabitants. The force of gravitation, being about one half what it is upon the earth, would enable a man weighing three or four hundred pounds to easily leap upwards to the height of five or six feet; this, in some emergencies, would doubtless be of advantage. Another thing to be noticed is, that navigation through the air must be made, upon this planet, the normal method of locomotion. One could swim through the atmosphere of Mars, if it has an atmosphere like that of the earth, as the inhabitants of the earth swim through the waters of the sea; this may be, however, a questionable advantage.

* Between Mars and Jupiter are twenty-three small bodies, called planetoids. They were formerly supposed to be parts of a planet thrown into fragments by some internal or external force; more likely is it that they have never been a single planet, but assumed their present dimensions when the fire-mist of the solar system crystallized, if this term may be allowed. Some of the planetoids can boast a diameter of considerable extent, though in no case over a few hundred miles, while others are not larger than a terrestrial mountain. We need not dwell upon their physical condition, as no one is disposed to assign to them inhabitants.

† Proctor.

But the following serious discomfitures must likewise be met with upon this planet. Its climate is far more rigorous than the earth's, its mass much less. It is doubtful if there is water upon it in quantities sufficient to produce a fog equal to that which, upon an autumn morning, hangs over a single American lake. The dark spots mapped out and named Phillips's Sea, Dawes's Ocean, and the like, are very far from being universally recognized as bodies of water.*

Seidel and Zöllner have arrived at the conclusion, after the most careful observations, that the light reflected from this planet comes, not, as in case of Jupiter and Saturn, from an envelope of clouds, but almost directly, as with the moon, from the true surface of the planet. Certain other scientists, who have given the subject not a little attention, claim that there is no satisfactory evidence that Mars has an atmosphere of sufficient consistency to support any form of organized physical life. Probabilities appear to be assuming the character of certainty, that Mars is already a worn-out world; its internal fires are nearly extinguished; its atmosphere and water are nearly absorbed; it has reached its perpetual autumn-brown hue, and is the home of utter desolation, like that which reigns upon the moon. With such facts and probabilities before us, is it not assumption to say that Mars is inhabitable? Nay more, with such facts

* For a long time the dark spots upon the moon were thought to be seas. "Sea of Serenity," "Sea of Crises," and "Sea of Humors," were some of the names given. It is useless to say the names have been dropped, and the former opinion discarded.

before us, and with the arguments from analogy and the consistency of things turned completely against the supporters of a plurality of inhabitable worlds, and brought to bear with all their force in support of the view that the earth alone is the seat of physical and organized life, is it not assumption, if not *presumption*, to say that Mars is inhabited? Faced by the facts gathered from every region of the physical universe, met by adverse analogies on the right hand and on the left, and confronted by the manifest import of revelation, we do not see how any one can have reasonable justification for saying that Mars is an inhabited planet until, at least, balloons can be descried rising in its atmosphere, or until ships can be seen sailing across its seas, or crowds be observed gathering at its seats of empire, or armies be beheld marshalling their hostile forces in settlement of international difficulties. Strong and decisive probabilities thus compel us to conclude that there is not a plurality of inhabited worlds in the physical universe. We turn, therefore, with all the more interest, to our *Earth*. We can say of it what we are able to say of no other spot in the universe — it is both inhabitable and inhabited. Scientific investigation shows with a remarkable degree of uniformity, as we have seen, that the solar system is the chief and the most complete of all similar systems, and also, that the earth is the only planet in the solar system known to have conditions essential to the existence of physical organisms; namely, land, water, and atmosphere, properly proportioned — "ground to stand upon, air to breathe, and water to nourish." The earth seems, therefore, if we mistake not, to be the one domesticated hearth-stone of the solar system. It holds a central position in the system to which it belongs; it occupies the temperate zone as to the other planets; upon the side next the sun are found the silence and desolation of worn-out worlds; upon the side opposite are worlds for the most part so fresh from the forge of the Infinite as to be but the abode of constant volcanic throes and eruptions. The earth seems to be the one arena God has selected, upon which to have wrought out some of the grandest problems that will ever be submitted to the universe.

The question, Why was this little earth chosen for such a purpose, instead of some object of vaster proportions, is quickly followed by a question equally pertinent: Why should it not have been chosen? It is as well adapted for the purpose of developing humanity and displaying the providence of God as any other world could be; it is large enough for that purpose, and has a history of sufficient duration. It is an objection of no weight to say that the sphere is too limited for an infinite God to bestow upon it such special attentions. For the physical universe, taken as a whole, is not infinite; * God must, there-

* This is easily shown. For if the sidereal system were infinite, then the whole heavens would shine with the brilliancy of starlight. This is very far from being the case. There are broad vacant spaces in the neighborhood of all nebulæ. "The access to the nebulæ," says Sir John Herschel, "is on all sides through a desert." Each one of these deserts reports that the stars, in number and distance, are finite.

fore bestow attention upon a part; it is for him to decide which that part shall be. The purposes of God cannot be safely estimated by rods and furlongs. The earth is large enough for him to display upon it infinite majesty, and the entire universe is to him a limitation.

Equally without force is the objection that God would not wait until a few thousand years ago before creating physical life. For why should he not wait? and besides this, since he is eternal, the objection lies with equal relevancy against any time that might have been selected; it was for him, and no one else, to decide the moment of time at which to call animate or inanimate creatures into being. Creation was a tardy moment, in a scientific point of view, whenever commenced or completed. But more than this, analogies and helps from every quarter come to our support in settlement of these various questions. Is it regarded as a needless consumption of time to employ countless ages in fitting up this earth for human abodes? Man is even yet a geological novelty in this world, whom no theory of development can account for. Myriads of years, also, and multitudes of different species of physical life appeared and disappeared long times before man came on earth to admire them. Was not such workmanship miscalculated and abortive? No one answers the question but with an emphatic No. Everybody feels that the divine glory and wisdom are not thereby brought into question. Nay, such delay and condescension do not dethrone the Infinite One. The Deity can lie concealed in a rose-bud without suffering dishonor. In the unsightly pool of muddy water he has ofttimes worked, precipitating therefrom the finest crystals and gems. What God has in store, and what he intends by present procedures, we cannot always tell; his ways are past finding out. He is in no haste. He works a twelvemonth to form a flower, which, unseen by human eye, withers the day it blooms. Some plants bud but once in a hundred years. He is likewise lavish of his expenditures even to apparent prodigality. He never minds a few score more than are wanted for a purpose. A million seeds fall from a tree when it is the arrangement for but one to take root; and the spawn of a single fish numbers two hundred millions. Of a truth, we are met here, there, and everywhere by assurances that it is in strict harmony with God's way to seem to waste his energies by hanging out this handsome "jewelry of the stars" innumerable, yet reserving but one of all the number for habitation. If it is ordered that the remaining part of the physical universe shall be but the leaves, the stems, the stocks of the one "fertile flower," or if it is planned that the earth shall be the one physical "sanctuary of the universe," "the Holy Land of Creation," the scene of God's special manifestation, the one, among a million others, around which the most vital interests are suspended, and connected with which the grandest issues are awaited; or if it is arranged that earthly humanity shall be the unique and peculiar child of the physical universe, and that the central point of the earth's history and of universal history, shall be, and is, the coming and life of man's elder brother, who lived in Nazareth; in fine, if the scientific and the physical centres of the universe shall be found to coincide with the theological centre as revealed in the Holy Scriptures, — even then no form of science need take the alarm, for such has been the way of the Infinite from the beginning.

The sublime truths of revealed religion, in view of these considerations, seem to find new expression, and come home to us with a wealth of suggestion heretofore unknown. The fundamental principles of Christianity hereby clear themselves from troublesome obscurities. We can the better understand why revelation places such high distinctions upon humanity, and why the entire gulfs of stars seem to pale almost into obscurity before one of the little ones whom our Saviour blessed: those children were not made for the stars, but the stars for them; and when every glistening sun shall fall from its place in the sky, the feeblest child shall continue to shine forth, and will shine forever and ever in the kingdom of heaven.

We see also why the Deity is so lavish of astronomical wonders in man's behalf; nothing short of stars enough to call out human thought and investigation until time ends, would be enough; it is as if God had said, "Anything I can do for man shall be done; give him extent of worlds to last him his lifetime, and sufficient to tax his skill and invention to the utmost." What if God has made the stars in number such that they appear as "silver sand" and "diamond dust;" he who has given us his Son, shall he not with him freely give us all things?

It is clear, also, why the present period, throughout the material universe is, so far as the nature of the case allows, the era of rest. It is God's Sabbath time.

The changes known to be taking place are not new creations; all things are pointing to decay and death. The workshop of the Almighty, his forge and productions, are cooling off; no sounds of the bellows or anvil are heard. It is as if, six thousand years ago, when humanity was brought forth, the Creator had commanded the intelligent universe to pause, and do nought else save to watch human development, and take note of the princes and kings as they shall prove themselves worthy of sceptres and thrones.

The consistency of things requires, also, that other changes respecting the arena of human development shall one day be wrought out. When man's earthly life terminates, the physical universe will have no further end to subserve; it shall be dissolved; * and then will have come the last epoch of the physical universe, and the story of its history and existence will have been told.† But in this dissolution are involved changes

* 2 Pet. iii. 10–13.

† The history of the physical universe can now be read with an accuracy scarcely less than that with which the geological history of the earth is examined. In general, "stellar geology," as the science is called, divides the history of the natural universe into the following periods: —

I. The Epoch of Light. Some part of the divine energy was at this period converted into perfect physical lumination, which was homogeneous, but which contained, perhaps, the elements or basis of the material part of the physical universe.

II. The Epoch of Mineral Mist. The mass of lumination passed into a degree of heterogeneousness; the solid light became points of light.

III. The Epoch of Condensation. The mineral mist, at this stage, became luminous liquid, with manifest tenden-

such as befit human destiny; universal decay and corruption are to put on incorruption; the earthy is to become heavenly, and the natural is to become spiritual.* Science has no word to speak against these changes. It is now shown that planets and suns, if suddenly arrested, would be converted into terrific conflagrations. Everything is now proved to be convertible into any or everything else. Heat and motion are interchangeable quantities. Diamonds and charcoal are equivalents. "Flowers are but earth vivified."†

cies towards assuming spherical forms, together with spiral motions.

IV. The Solar Epoch. The liquid mass became of such consistency as to shape itself into globes of solid fire, surrounded by a blazing photosphere; the largest body in a given system becoming the centre of an organized system of worlds.

V. The Planetary Epoch. This may be subdivided into three stages. (1.) The preparatory stage. The luminous fires were extinguished; periodic revolution was established; crusts formed; waters fell as now upon Jupiter, and later as during the earth's period of rain; and geological history was brought on towards completion. (2.) The stage of culmination. This stage presents all the phases of physical geography, as now displayed upon the earth. (3.) The stage of desolation. The internal fires are completely or nearly extinguished; the waters and atmosphere are absorbed, and the period of utter darkness and universal refrigeration is ushered in.

VI. We add upon Bible authority the Epoch of Spiritualization. The physical universe will be arrested in its motion by the hand that first gave it movement; instantly every orb will be again in flames; all things will be changed in a moment, and in the twinkling of an eye; and the physical universe will be succeeded by the spiritual.

* 1 Cor. xv. 46, 49, 53.

† Lamartine.

"And I saw a new heaven and a new earth: for the first heaven and the first earth were passed away; and there was no more sea. And I John saw the holy city, new Jerusalem, coming down from God out of heaven, prepared as a bride adorned for her husband. And I heard a great voice out of heaven, saying, Behold, the tabernacle of God is with men, and he will dwell with them, and they shall be his people, and God himself shall be with them, and be their God. And God shall wipe away all tears from their eyes; and there shall be no more death, neither sorrow, nor crying, neither shall there be any more pain; for the former things are passed away." *

* Rev. xxi. 1-4.

THE DEFEAT.

His eye no more looked onward, but its gaze
Rests where remorse a life misspent surveys.
By the dark shape of what he *is*, serene
Stands the bright ghost of what he might have been;
Here the vast loss, and there the worthless gain, —
Vice scorned, yet wooed, and Virtue loved in vain.

BULWER.

What more, O Avarice, canst thou do to us,
Since thou my blood so to thyself hast drawn,
It careth not for its own proper flesh? DANTE.

"Little sins are pioneers of hell."

The sea of this world hides so many rocks that a vessel whose rudder is not in the hand of Wisdom must of necessity soon suffer shipwreck. HENGSTENBERG.

The great art of life is to play for much and stake but little.

JOHNSON.

Sin is a sweet poison; it tickleth while it stabbeth. The first thing that sin doth is to bewitch, then to put out the eyes, then to take away the sense and feeling; to do to a man as Lot's daughters did to him, make him drunk, and then he doth he knoweth not what. As Joab came with a kind salute to Abner and thrust him under the fifth rib, while Abner thought of nothing but kindness, so sin comes smiling, comes pleasing and humoring thee, while it giveth thee a deadly stab. ANTHONY BURGESS.

No man can be stark nought at once. Let us stop the progress of sin in our soul at the first stage, for the farther it goes the faster it will increase. FULLER.

As sins proceed they ever multiply, and like figures in arithmetic, the last stands for more than all that went before it. SIR THOMAS BROWNE.

My lord cardinal [Cardinal Richelieu], there is one fact which you seem to have entirely forgotten. God is a sure paymaster. He may not pay at the end of the week, month, or year; but I charge you remember that he pays in the end.
ANNE OF AUSTRIA.

Nothing is more common than for great thieves to ride in triumph where small ones are punished. But let wickedness escape as it may, at the last it never fails of doing itself justice; for every guilty person is his own hangman. SENECA.

In general, treachery, though at first sufficiently cautious, yet in the end betrays itself. LIVY.

Extreme avarice almost always makes mistakes. There is no passion that oftener misses its aim, nor on which the present has so much influence in prejudice of the future.
ROCHEFOUCAULD.

Use sin as it will use you; spare it not, for it will not spare you; it is your murderer and the murderer of the whole world. Use it, therefore, as a murderer should be used; kill it before it kills you; and though it bring you to the grave, as it did your head, it shall not be able to keep you there. You love not death; love not the cause of death. BAXTER.

Suicide is a crime most revolting to the feelings; nor does any reason suggest itself to our understanding by which it can be justified. NAPOLEON.

THE DEFEAT.

EVERY man's life ends in defeat or triumph. Those who suffer final defeat may have gained, meantime, some single and signal victories; while those who achieve a final triumph may have met, early in the contest, many a rough defeat.

Illustrative of each of these classes we take two characters, familiar to all readers of the Sacred Scriptures, both of which are as apt examples for our purpose as any others therein recorded.

Judas, the apostate, is a name, as it seems to us, synonymous with the word *defeat*. Little is known of his early life; so little, indeed, that nothing can be said. This is true of almost every biblical character. We find the various contestants in Scripture history struggling in their vigorous manhood; in that struggle, and not in their birth, or their youth, is involved their final defeat or triumph, though birth and youth may have had much to do therewith.*

* Legend tells us that Judas was a foredoomed wretch, whose mother received a warning of what he would be, in a dream, before his birth. To avoid this, his parents enclosed him in a chest, and plunged him into the sea. The sea cast

After the mere mention of the name of Judas, and his call to the apostleship, he comes first into notice at a festival in Bethany, at the house of Simon the leper. The circumstances attending this gathering are of interest. It was the evening of the day on which our Lord had arrived in that village from a season of retirement in the country near Ephraim. The inhabitants of Bethany were filled with delight, "and," says the sacred record, "there they made him a supper." It was similar to the complimentary entertainments of modern times given in honor of distinguished guests. This effort on the part of these humble people was an expression of hearts beating with love and adoration for a friend who was more than brother.

Of those present some are specially worthy of mention. He, for instance, who was master of the house, Simon, bearing the surname "Leper." He had once been afflicted with that terrible disease, which no physician could heal. He had been obliged to utter the mournful cry, "Unclean, unclean!" as a warning to

him upon the shore in the domain of a king and queen, who adopted him as their own son. Malignant from his birth, he killed a foster-brother, and fled to Judea, and became a page to Pontius Pilate. He committed many monstrous crimes, was at length filled with contrition and terror, and fled to Christ for peace. Thenceforward the account agrees with the New Testament narrative. After the betrayal, despair came and offered him choice of weapons of destruction, and he chose the rope and hung himself. At his death his evil genius seized the broken rope, and dragged him down to the seething abyss below. At his approach hell sent forth a shout of joy. Lucifer smoothed his pain-racked brow, and from his burning throne welcomed a greater sinner than himself.

those who approached him. But upon the night in question he was a well man. The ugly spots had gone, and his skin was like that of a child. A monument was he and a glad witness for Him who had pronounced the almighty words, "*Be clean.*"

There was another person in the guest chamber especially deserving mention. He was a young man who, a few months before this, had been enshrouded and borne to the tomb, surrounded by his weeping sisters and a sympathizing community. No citizen of Bethany doubted his death and burial. But in obedience to a single command from his divine Friend, he came forth from the tomb; the aspect of death had disappeared; the breeze from the hill-side blew off the smell of the grave; and he returned with his friends, and helped remove from his home the symbols and emblems of his own funeral. And with all these things Judas was perfectly familiar.

The presence of Mary, the sister of Lazarus, at this entertainment, cannot be overlooked, for she played no unimportant part.* Entering the chamber during the festivities, she quietly approached the one in whose honor the feast was spread. Gratitude, veneration, and love were in her heart. At a moment when least observed, the devoted woman broke the seal of a well-closed alabaster box of pure oil of spikenard, very costly; with lavish hand she poured the whole of it upon the head of Jesus, and upon his feet, and then knelt and wiped his feet with her loosened tresses. The house was filled with fragrance. This

* Matt. xxvi. 6-9. Mark xiv. 3-5. John xii. 2-4.

tribute was more suggestive than Mary knew. It appears upon the surface to be an act of gratitude done by a simple-hearted, loving woman, to one who had pardoned her sins, told her of heaven, and raised to life her dead brother; but it was more than that. It was also a prophetic tribute; it was a memorial, which, wherever the gospel is preached, shall be told of her. In all the remotest regions of the world, and in the latest ages of time, this shall be told, that Jesus died "in the fragrant odors of this dear woman's love."

But one there was in that company who did not enjoy the fragrance of spikenard. There are such, — those, we mean, who enjoy nothing unless inaugurated by themselves, or unless it contributes directly to their desires or purposes. With such very little in this world is exactly right; no morning is without its cloud, and the most finished picture is a daub, and the whitest marble has its flaws. How little such men suspect that the flaw is in their own souls! How much like the waves of the troubled sea do hearts like that of Judas cast up mire and dirt!

This dissatisfied and restless man quickly, but quietly and artfully, circulated among his fellow-disciples the plausible inquiry, "Why was not this ointment sold for three hundred pence, and given to the poor? *

By his remarkable power of eloquence, his profound respect for religion, his reverence for the teachings of the Master, his sober conversation, together with his plausible address, his unbounded sympathy and benev-

* John xii. 5.

olent appeal, Judas inaugurated disaffection, and completely misled the body of the disciples. For the moment they were fastened in the same snare that held him, and we hear them also inquiring, "To what purpose is this waste? for this ointment might have been sold for much, and given to the poor." "And they murmured against her." * How successfully had this festal scene been converted into an hour of temptation, and the pure offering of a loving heart into an offence!

But Jesus was moved by this act of the woman. Of himself and the dishonor done him personally by these murmurings he said nothing; it grieved him to the quick, nevertheless, that the woman had been so badly and unkindly used; like a faithful advocate he appeared at once in her defence. "Trouble her not," he said, "for this" (following the original) "is a beautiful work which she hath wrought." †

Such were the gentle words which silenced the

* Matt xxvi. 8, 9. Mark xiv. 6, 9.

† Matt. xxvi. 10–13. Mark xiv. 6–9. John xii. 7, 8. Alford makes an excellent observation upon this prophecy of Christ. "We cannot but be struck with the majesty of this prophetic announcement, introduced with the peculiar and weighty ἀμὴν λέγω ὑμῖν, conveying, by implication, the whole mystery of the εὐαγγέλιον which should go forth from his death, as its source, looking forward to the end of time, when it shall have been preached in the whole world, and specifying the fact that this deed should be recorded wherever it is preached." He sees in this announcement a distinct prophetic recognition of the existence of *written* gospel records, by means of which alone the deed related could be universally proclaimed.

murmurings of the disciples, or changed them into praise and compliment, and fully restored confidence to the distressed woman's heart. But he who had occasioned this disturbance was exasperated; he felt, without the least occasion for it, that a personal wrong had been done him; in consequence, he began at once to dally with thoughts of treachery, and took the preliminary steps in the ways of treason.

He was likewise much provoked because he had not so well succeeded as he had planned. Something, of course, is wrong upon the face of his transactions. His conduct and words were the expression of benevolence, but his heart appears to be the home of selfishness. The inspired writer leaves us not long in doubt, but explores and explodes, in a word, this pretended piety and professed regard for the poor, and gives us a clew by which henceforth we may follow this sower of dissensions: "This he said, not that he cared for the poor, but because he was a thief, and had the bag, and bare what was put therein." * This man had been preaching up benevolence, it thus appears, with the hidden intention of making something handsome out of it for himself. Of such perfidy was his heart fully capable. This apostle was simply a hypocrite. He had shown talent, he had exerted a controlling influence, but it is ordained from the beginning that a hypocrite cannot long triumph in his hypocrisy. As Judas withdrew we discover that defeat already has been written upon his leading purpose. Iniquity gains much, but rarely the thing wanted, and never the thing best.

* John xii. 6.

Now fairly introduced to Judas, we may follow him a step farther. Jerusalem is west of Bethany a distance of a trifle less than two miles, the Mount of Olives standing between. Thither Judas, as he left the feast chamber, directed his steps. As he reached the summit of the Mount of Olives, the scene under the clear sky and full moon of that evening must have been enchanting. At the foot of the mount, looking westward, was the valley of Jehoshaphat; beyond was Jerusalem; to the south of the city lay the valley of Hinnom, which, extending east and west, united with the valley of Jehoshaphat at a point south-east of the city. The bluffs on either side these valleys, at their junction, are from twenty-five to forty feet in height. In the time of our Saviour they were in excellent state of cultivation, and richly clothed with vineyards and olive trees. On the left, passing up Hinnom, was the Hill of Evil Counsel, on which was the Potters' Field, afterwards purchased with the thirty bloody pieces of silver. Opposite this, towards the city, in full view from the position we now occupy on the summit of the Mount of Olives, was a spot of land which was replete with interest to Judas; he owned it. He paused to look upon it a moment before descending to the city. He might have reasoned thus: That is mine. What if Christ and his other followers go to wreck and ruin; I am safe. Let them waste the ointment if they like; that spot of land will support me.

Indeed, that was a choice lot, one of the best in the environs of the entire city. It commanded a view of both these important valleys referred to; it looked upon Mount Zion, the Mount of Olives, and two other important elevations, since known as the Mounts of Offence and Evil Counsel; it was at that time plentifully irrigated by water drawn from the Pool of Siloam. Yes, Judas was a sharp, shrewd man, and a sharp, shrewd buyer. No one could overreach him, and no good bargain in Jerusalem would escape his notice. He was a provident man, as the world would say; in case of a failure on the part of Christ and his mission, Judas had taken the precaution to make these suitable provisions for himself and family.*

And notice, that these ample provisions had been made even though the conditions of discipleship required that all things should be given up, — real estate with personal property, — and the whole turned over into the common treasury. It had proved perilous in one instance, at least, not to do this much.† But Judas had done much worse; he was not only a deceiver and a hypocrite, but a defaulter; he was a thief; nay, the worst kind of a thief. The gifts of friends, in some instances the gifts of poor people, given to Jesus by way of expressing their love, intrusted to Judas, the treasurer of the company, — even these he had purloined from the bag, and with this doubly consecrated money had purchased this splendid suburban estate, to which he could retire when the mission of Jesus was accomplished.‡ But all this

* The psalm supposed to be written descriptive of the betrayer mentions the fact of both wife and children. — Psalm cix. Acts i. 20.

† Acts v. 1–12.

‡ "Now this man purchased a field with the reward of iniquity." Acts i. 18. This was purchased, not with the money

could not have been so successfully accomplished unless Judas had been far above the average of men. No one could have managed his affairs as these were managed, have covered up his steps with such skilful tact, and have escaped the suspicion of every one of his companions, even to the last, of being anything other than a man of superior devotion and unquestioned integrity, unless by the aid of positive intellectual ability. It always takes about twice the amount of brains to gain an end dishonestly that it does to gain it honestly.

Judas was also perfectly self-confident, yet with a show of modesty. He was smart; he knew it. He had his abilities under perfect self-control, and always, somehow, skilfully managed them in his own personal interest.

By universal consent the money was intrusted entirely to his care and disposal; his accounts were, perhaps, never questioned or audited. His hand was always upon the sails when they needed reefing. His ability would have been acknowledged and his influence instantly felt in any position. Public responsibility, from which others shrank, he would have easily borne. His occasional pilfering and thieving tended to make him more and more subtle, shrewd, artful, and cautious. He never allowed himself to be pent up or

which was thrown at the feet of the priests in the temple; that went to buy the Potters' Field, on the Mount of Evil Counsel (Matt. xxvii. 6–10); but this field opposite was the purchase of money stolen. We can now see why, at the supper in Bethany, this man had pleaded so zealously for the poor.

hemmed into close quarters, such that his genius could find no way out. No one plays the Judas adroitly and to the purpose unless he is a man of much mind. Common men become petty villains; real talent will not stoop to steal old junk or clothes-pins; it strikes rather for the most that can be reached.

Does it not sometimes appear that those men and women of any community who are serving the tables of worldly pleasure with the greatest devotion are more talented than those who are in the service of the church? This is not always the case; but frequently does it not so appear? The smartest men everywhere are the meanest. Had the talents of some of the lewdest women been consecrated to God, they would, by universal consent, have occupied the first ranks in society.

But it is well to note that bad men, who are very smart, are very far from smart in one thing — this, that they do not see that it is exceedingly foolish and short-sighted to do wrong instead of right. The cheat smiles that he has cheated another, not thinking how fearfully he has cheated himself. How cheaply most such sell themselves! "Smart, but foolish," is an epitaph suitable for more gravestones than one.

Notice another thing. Judas was never rash, like the other disciples, but always cool and self-collected. He wore, perhaps, no better clothes than did his companions, but was, we suspect, always in better trim. He was one of those slick, smooth men, who ever have for you a smile; but it is well not to take too much stock in some men's smiles; a man's face is part of his stock in trade. The affability of Judas afforded a cloak of completest protection. The wolf could be detected by no ordinary observation. He was so agreeable and apparently disinterested, that half the world, for want of better discernment, would have thought him the politest of gentlemen. He knew in all company how best to deport himself. His want of gallantry was completely veiled under a hypocritical display of manners. Politeness is genuine kindness of heart; of this Judas was utterly destitute. He was as ungentlemanly as he was base. He could cast, without hesitation, a burden of disquietude and confusion upon the spirit of that devoted woman who honored Christ with her costly sacrifice. Was that politeness? What cared he for Mary's heart? It was only a few ounces of flesh. If he had broken it or crushed it to atoms, while clutching for the three hundred pence, it would not have troubled him. Such affable men, wherever met, are not gentlemen. When the poor woman and the shop-worn girl cry out that their hearts and lives are crushed between the pavement and the feet of that man who in many a circle passes for a gentleman, nothing more need be said; God's judgment cannot give a more inevitable lie to all such false pretensions. One who abuses another is not a gentleman; one who lives on other folks' money, or lives extravagantly, if he does not pay his debts, is not a gentleman; nay, one who in any way appropriates to his own use what belongs to another is not a gentleman; he is a reckless-man.

We parted company with Judas upon the Mount of Olives, where he was congratulating himself upon his successful transactions. Under his eye was that magnificent plot of ground; let us look well to *that plot of ground*, for we shall have sad and special occasion to revisit it anon.

It must have been quite late, perhaps near midnight, when Judas reached the outer gate, upon the eastern side of the city. Making known his mission to the guard, he was at once admitted, and accompanied to the temple. At that hour silence reigned in all its outer courts. The cloisters and halls which, during the day, were thronged with worshippers, were now deserted and empty. The night wind swept through those cloistered aisles, meeting nought unusual save this one restless and sleepless adventurer. The watch-stars from above seemed to look down upon this solitary visitant with strange inquiries. The moon was in her full, and the sky was cloudless. How sublimely grand must the temple have then appeared to this disciple of Jesus! The great blocks of fine white marble were joined together with such perfect skill that no seam could be traced. The building had the appearance of having been cut into its present shape out of one solid block of marble. In the distance, on approaching the city, it resembled a mountain of snow. How imposing the sight to this one, who for three years had dwelt with Him who was more homeless than the bird of the air and the fox of the hill-side.

Over the porch of the court of the priests, encircling the pillars, was a vine made of solid gold, hung with golden grapes, whose clusters were of the size of a man. Heavy plates of gold covered this entrance to the temple, reflecting the moonlight, and making every object visible. Look now upon this defaulter and intentional betrayer, as he passed through those empty but majestic temple courts; he entered at the gate called, Beautiful; he had often entered it before; he proceeded onward through the Court of the Gentiles, and up the nineteen steps to the Court of the Israelites, where he asked audience of the priests then on duty. They proffered him immediate hearing, and he was requested to make known his mission. He broke the silence with the question, "What will ye give me, and I will deliver him unto you?" Ah, that was a fatal question. It was a rough, heartless, slave-vender's question. This man hucksters for a price upon the head of the priceless. He barters for blood. "And when they heard it," says Mark, "they were glad." Glad! What a beautiful word! How it wells up from childhood! Soiled henceforth is that word.

What had troubled these men was this: they feared the common people. They could not arrest Christ except in their absence. They therefore needed for a guide one who was well acquainted with all the private resorts of our Saviour; here was their man. How providential? An uproar among the people can now be prevented. They deliberated, gave explanations, and offered thirty pieces of silver.

Doubtless for such signal service Judas had expected a much larger sum. But they made it clear to him why they could not consistently give more than the price stipulated. They did not wish to recognize in Christ anything but the meanest specimen of humanity. The current price of a common slave was thirty pieces of silver.* Judas saw the force of their

* About fifteen dollars.

reasoning. He was helped likewise to see the force of other things. He felt, doubtless, that all hope of promotion, should he remain with the company of the disciples, was at an end. His Master would neither employ the enthusiasm of the people nor his miraculous powers to secure temporal position. Why follow him longer? *

Judas also remembered the slight he had received; and his peculiar estimate of such a slight would not allow him to brook it. He felt, for the moment, as he ascended those temple steps, that he was not the man to receive a personal rebuff from that Nazarene, whom the devil made him now look upon, not as the Messiah, but as only a Rabbi.

In addition to this, the scene at Bethany presented to his mind only a wasteful company, in which all things were going to dissolution. Those former dreams

* The heart of Judas had probably been not exactly right from the beginning, and his talents were consequently useless for any great purpose. It is only sanctified talent that is better than no talent. The less a wicked man knows, the better. The appearance of Christ, the glory of his marvellous deeds, and the expectation of universal dominion subject to his control, had attracted this man from Kerioth. He made an accurate estimate of those things. "He swore fealty to the *banner*, but not to the *humiliation*, of Christ." Judas may not at first have been consciously a hypocrite. He very likely for a time played the part of a disciple with a commendable degree of outward and inward truthfulness. He probably did not at first pretend much more than did others. He, with others, followed Jesus politically, and with no deeper or higher motives than a longing for the realization of those earthly and enchanting ideas which his lively imagination had depicted to him.

of his had been dashed to the ground. Now, here, in the temple, was the place and the opportunity for restoring what seemed lost. With these rulers, with whom he was holding this midnight interview, was authority, which his Master seemed not to have; wealth and power were there, but belonged not to his Master. He thought, too, that his Master was terribly extravagant. To a man constituted like Judas he did ofttimes seem thus. It was not at the Bethany supper alone that the avarice of Judas had discovered what seemed to be, on the part of our Saviour, a needless and careless expenditure of property, but elsewhere he had seen the same thing without understanding its purport. He saw property wasted as if it had cost nothing, and since it was being squandered so carelessly, why could he not take his share?

Besides all this, he had estimated his own talents. He had reckoned that as he was of more service to the Master than the rest of his followers, he was consequently entitled to extra compensation. No burden was so great and important as his. Why should he not receive somewhat extra therefor? and by making these appropriations quietly, instead of publicly, he could prevent, on the part of his fellow-disciples, all complaint. There was policy in his method, and also justice, as he thought. Three years had been wasted. Three years were of value to him. If, then, his hopes of promotion were gone, might he not still remain and pocket what he could? By taking only half the receipts he would save to the Master more than any one else. Might he not turn his own receipts to as good use as any one else? Thus, in a hundred and one ways, Judas had been quieting his conscience and excusing himself, until he could frame an excuse for the most daring impiety. So can any man. But the old adage tells us a plain truth. He that *excuses* himself in any act is at the same moment his own *accuser*.

Self-excusing and the grand scenes surrounding Judas had thus accomplished their work. He was mentally intoxicated; rather exhilarated. How insignificant the festal chamber in Bethany, in comparison with what then blinded his eye and tempted his heart! There, in that temple and with those priests, were wealth and power. Those temple officials guarded immense treasures; thousands were nothing to them, while small amounts of money for present needs, the gifts of charity, which could be carried from place to place in a bag, constituted his Master's possessions. If not now, the time may come, he reasoned, when these men and their wealth will be of service; I shall be their guest in all the future; * my standing as a citizen depends upon breaking from Jesus, and forming a confederacy with these rulers. His silence in view of their proposition became oppressive. Each minute's delay seemed an hour. Why delay? Yes, Judas, why delay? Take the thirty pieces; they will be all you *can* receive, and all the priests will give; for these are the words of the old prophet: "So they weighed for my price thirty pieces of silver." †

* In this Judas must take his chances; they are, under like circumstances, more often adverse than otherwise. Hail fellows are not always well met.

† Zech. xi. 12. In view of what has now been said, the

With these terms the bargain was closed, and Jesus was sold for exactly one third the price of the ointment, by the very man who grumbled against the woman who had poured it as an anointing upon the devoted head of our Saviour; whilst if Judas could have sold that offering of devotion, he would have stolen its price, have added it to his other thefts, and then have absconded with the whole.

The next scene to which the inspired writers introduce us is in a guest-chamber in the city of Jerusalem. The time was the evening of the first day of unleavened bread; consequently four days have intervened since we left the festal scene in Bethany. How that time was passed by Judas we are not informed. Upon this evening the Bethany friends of our Lord did not appear. Martha was not needed to serve the Master, nor Mary to anoint him, nor Lazarus and Simon to witness for him; these services had been already well performed. None but his disciples were present. We first look in upon a supper which preceded the institution of the Lord's Supper; no chair was at that time vacant; no face was especially downcast; from present appearances one would suspect no lurking wrong. But a man was there who had already bargained to sell his Master for the price of a *slave*.

point raised by Story, that the bribe was too small to move Judas, seems answered. It is stated thus: —

"Does not the bribe seem all too small and mean?
He held the common purse, and, were he thief,
Had daily power to steal, and lay aside
A secret and accumulating fund;
So doing, he had nothing risked of fame,
While here he braved the scorn of all the world."

How Judas could have braved it sufficiently to come, after that transaction in the temple, sit down with his Master, and eat the paschal supper, as if nothing were in his heart but good intentions and wishes, is almost beyond conjecture. But he was a man of consummate coolness.*

Pictures representing the "Lord's Supper" present twelve disciples with their Master. One sitting near our Lord is represented of dark complexion, having a morose expression, mingled with satanic hate and revenge. These representations involve two important mistakes. First, there were but eleven disciples at the Lord's Supper. This feast of which we are now speaking was a preliminary entertainment, — the paschal supper, at which Judas was present; he retired before the institution of the Lord's Supper. Second, he wore, on that occasion, anything but a malignant face. We doubt if he was of dark complexion. No one smiled more frequently, conversed more freely, appeared easier in his movements, or occasioned less suspicion among his fellows.

As treasurer of the company, and on account of his commanding influence, Judas took a position next the Master, a privilege that none disputed. With a trifling

* We say, without entering into any lengthy discussion, that the presence of Judas at this supper table, after the transaction with the priests in the temple, betokens as heartless perfidy, as diabolical hypocrisy and treachery as can be found on record; and those who have attempted to palliate the guilt of Judas — De Quincey and Archbishop Whately, for illustration — have in nothing else been more unsuccessful. See also Appendix G.

difference growing out of the question among certain others, in which Judas was in no wise engaged, as to "who shall be the greatest," which was easily silenced by our Saviour, the scene, at first, was one of *apparent* joy and happiness. But a cloud rested, during this interview, upon the mind of our Saviour. He knew the whole; the past and the future were fully disclosed to his eye, as were, likewise, all the hearts in that company; and he knew, among other things, that there was one of that number who was, and had been, at heart a devil.

Pertinent, perhaps, is the question, at this point, Who made Judas to differ from his fellow-disciples? There can be but one reply. God makes men intellectually and circumstantially different, but the use each one makes of his talents and surroundings involves in every case personal responsibility. God gave Judas superior abilities, but, contrary to his deeper convictions of right and duty, he prostituted them. Clearly, then, he was responsible. His natural ability was such as to raise him very high or sink him very low. The antithesis of character is left, ultimately, to personal choice. There had been offered to each disciple the same gospel; each had felt the Spirit's influence; each had possessed the same gracious opportunities; the world, the flesh, and the devil had addressed the heart of each; each, in fine, had been subjected to peculiar temptations and peculiar allurements. But the other disciples had chosen Christ, and commenced their ascent to heaven; this reprobate had chosen the world, and had descended, and was continuing to descend to the kingdom of Satan.

What is true in these instances is true of all others. All men are responsible parties in every transaction. No one can shift his responsibility upon any one else. There is no man, however low he has fallen, but knows, whatever his case may be to-day, that the time has been when he could have, and when he felt he ought to have, chosen the path of holiness and heaven. Our antecedents certainly have much to do with us; but despite antecedents, we can resist the devil if we will; in that are involved the sublimest resistance and grandest conquest. Some of those whose antecedents have been as black as one can well picture, have been governed by purposes based upon the highest integrity, and have, nevertheless, become the most honored instruments in God's service. Moral differences are always optional; else we are not men, but machines. Tremendous, therefore, are the powers intrusted to every man; and great is the fall of that man's house who builds upon sand.

The day had been when, in the innocence of childhood, Judas had sported on the hills of Kerioth, which were almost within sight from the Mount of Olives. He was the hope and confidence of parents and friends. A promising youth he must have been. But he had one point of danger and exposure. Satan could overthrow him, if at all, by bringing everything to bear upon that point; and at that point, without a double guard, Satan could overthrow him. But Judas, in this respect, was no worse than others. Every man has his weak point of character; some one where and respecting one thing; others another where and respecting something else. It has come to be an adage that every man has his price, at which Satan can buy him. And Satan knows enough not to make great bids for small returns. He can better afford to plot twenty years for the overthrow of a great soul than contrive a single day to entangle one who is not much. Luther, Paul, our Saviour, what assaults they received! When one is severely tempted by the devil, a compliment is paid. The devil strikes *only*, we were about to say, for the best; he seems to let the half-wits go; but Christ strikes for all, rank and file; * to him all souls are equally dear and alike precious.

The basis of an avaricious character was born in Judas; this was his weakness, — his easily besetting sin, — and Satan knew it. Properly controlled, however, and sanctified, this disposition would have proved a benefit to the world and the church. It would have led him to gather up the fragments, that nothing be lost, that the whole might be consecrated to God. As it was, however, this element of character became the source of danger; he kept yielding until avarice became a ruling passion. It was love of *gain* that kept him from going back, when "many went back, and walked no more with him" (Christ).

* But the results are widely opposite in the two opposite cases. Those who accept Christ, he inspires with his own life, and they at length are able to confound the unsanctified wisdom of the world. Those of many accomplishments, on the other hand, whom the devil deceives, he at length plunges into disgrace and ruin. It is thus that the first often become last, and the last first. In the end God will have the best troops in the field, and will keep in advance of Satan.

It was not carrying the bag while he followed the Master, but, at length, following the Master that he might carry the bag and pilfer from it, that made Judas a thief and a hireling. He might have carried the bag with the same devotion that others carried the cross, if he had been so disposed. It was, doubtless, however, a very hazardous thing for Judas to hear the clink of coin, when he saw that all hope of promotion from the position of bag-carrier among that company of Galileans to the emoluments of lord high treasurer of the new kingdom of Israel, was at an end. As he saw Christ, day by day, yielding up every opportunity of establishing a kingdom, and of gratifying the golden hopes of his followers, and as he began to suspect that Christ's kingdom was not to be temporal, but spiritual (which fact seemed to have been apprehended by Judas sooner than by any other disciple), the money was no longer safe in his hands. Some men are so constituted that they had better never expose themselves to the dangers and temptations of handling other men's money. Such was Judas, and many other such there are who had better seek other employment. Much depends upon adaptation between employment and constitutional characteristics. If a man puts himself in the teeth of danger, the chances are, that in the same hour of his venture, occasions, impulses, and circumstances will conspire against him; and unless there is a double guard at the point of weakness, also the defence of previous resistance, the victim is surely ruined; then shall be seen, not what a day, but what an hour and even a moment, can bring forth.

Pertinent, also, is another question: Why was Judas selected for this position, and why was he allowed to hold it, if Christ knew all? * Truly it seems a terrible dispensation by which God did, in this case, and does, also, in other cases, allow wicked men to minister in holy things. How strange that a wolf dressed in black is allowed sometimes to occupy a pulpit! But is any injustice done such characters if God does not at once strike them with a thunderbolt, rather than leave them to a gradual exposure and a no less terrible doom? In the instance before us, we suspect that Judas was hardly selected for the place he filled, but that he got himself the place. He was an office-seeker, the last, of all men, fit for office, but the men who somehow often obtain the office they desire. God allowed such disposal of events eighteen hundred years ago, and allows it still.

But why allow Judas to hold the position? We do not know. This case of Judas is only one of a thousand. The moment any defaulter commences his course, why does not Providence arrest his steps or depose him from

* Story states this point strongly: —

"Besides, why chose they for their almoner
A man so lost to shame, so foul with greed?
Or why, from some five-score of trusted men,
Choose him as one apostle among twelve?
Or why, if he were known to be so vile
(And who can hide his baseness at all times?),
Keep him in close communion to the last?
Nought in his previous life, or acts, or words,
Shows this consummate villain, that, full-grown,
Leaps all at once to such a height of crime."

his position of trust? It does not. Our Saviour did in the case of Judas as God now often does in the case of sinful men; he employed all possible means to win back the rebel heart, though knowing full well that none of them would avail. Events must be so ordered that every mouth shall be stopped in the day of judgment, and all things will then disclose that God has done the best he could under the circumstances, in every individual case, to bless and redeem.

It would, of course, have been just for Christ abruptly to have exposed this traitor, and have disgraced him in the presence of his fellow-disciples. But he did not. He treated him kindly. What could have succeeded if not kindness? He knelt, at their last meeting but one, and bathed that disciple's feet. How could Judas have escaped, at that moment, a twinge of remorse? Peter, under his personal sense of unworthiness, exclaimed, as our Lord approached him with towel and bowl, "Thou shalt never wash my feet." But this complacent hypocrite, defaulter, and traitor allowed the act without objection or hesitation.

He was also admitted into the nearest and most intimate relationship. He was intrusted with the most important office. What, that could be, was not done for Judas? He listened daily to the instructions, counsels, and prayers of his Master. Some of the teachings of our Lord were presented in such a way as seemingly to have been given especially to overcome the constitutional failing of Judas. The contrast between the service of God and Mammon, the discourse on the deceitfulness of riches, the proverb of the camel and the eye of the needle, the parable of the rich but

man, and the requirements made
ruler, must have fallen upon this m
.igh they had been chiefly or solely
If he would have yielded to the tr
rcumstances, it would have been \
ited with Christ; but men are somet
:he steps of the temple. It was not
las, because he was treasurer, to betra
Ie did that voluntarily. Those talei
ey been consecrated, — there was no r
iould not have been, —would have im
nd have given him one of the highes
; his fellows. Yes, everything was
be done, in consistency with his freedc
ayward disciple, but he would not; tl
aside from no injustice done, there
urpose in allowing Judas to pursue
old his position. He thereby becam
Christ had permitted to remain amor
even after repeated thefts. He was
ut the world's witness to the integrit
f this company which was led by Jesus
een fraud anywhere, it would hav
epartment of the treasury. If Christ
postor, he would have winked at cei
es, and have connived with his *treasu*
harp-eyed, shrewd man, the sharpe
dest of the twelve, at length confes
that Jesus was faultless and pure.
l, was it, if Judas was bent upon a
, that he had been permitted to carr
araoh was he in accomplishing divine

The wrath of man will always work out the praise of God. God rules, the devil tries to.

"And as they did eat," continues the narrative, "Jesus said, Behold, the hand of him that betrayeth me is with me on the table." * Eleven of that company were terror-struck; one only remained cool and self-composed. They looked upon one another in amazement. The question flew from mouth to mouth, "Lord, is it I?" "Is it I?" "Is it I?" † No one there bore the face of a traitor. Each, for the moment, thought not of his neighbor, but of himself.‡ Yet that man, who knew more than the others, who had already agreed to the betrayal, remained silent, and doubtless his fellow-disciples mistook his silence for conscious integrity.

Our Lord, perceiving that no effect was produced upon the insensibility of Judas by this indefinite intimation, and being still desirous of reaching his heart, narrowed the group, and said, "He that dippeth his hand with me in the dish, the same shall betray me." § And still we read that "the disciples looked one on another, doubting of whom he spake." But Judas had meanwhile unwittingly betrayed himself, by an act which seems to have been unobserved by any of his fellow-disciples.

The Master, it is well known, was the proper dispenser of the food at the table. But, in an unguarded moment, Judas had dipped in the dish where no one

* Matt. xxvi. 21, 22. Mark xiv. 18, 19. Luke xxii. 21, 23. John xiii. 21, 22.

† Matt. xxvi. 22. Mark xiv. 19.

‡ John xiii. 22.

§ Matt. xxvi. 23.

else would have, and where no other one save the Master ought to have dipped the ladle. It was an accident. Judas did not intend to be discourteous. He meant to have received the portion allotted to him, as did the others; but unconsciously the speaking hand betrayed the traitor,* and forthwith our Saviour added, "The Son of man indeed goeth, as it is written of him, but woe to the man by whom the Son of man is betrayed! Good were it for *that man* if he had never been born." †

What an appalling denunciation! Kind invitations and offices having failed, our Lord sought to awaken the slumbering conscience of this follower by tearing from before his eyes the mask with which Satan had so successfully blinded him.

Why stands not Judas pale as a corpse?

How heedlessly men sometimes thrust aside the de-

* "It is a psychological fact," says Lange, "that an evil conscience will betray itself in the hand, at the very moment when one succeeds in showing a hypocritical face, full of innocence and calmness."

Mr. Webster was once examining a witness, whose story, under direct and cross examination, had been unusually clear and explicit. There was no deviation, in sentence or word. The testimony could not be broken or impeached. The witness was perfectly composed, and his voice not the least tremulous. But Mr. Webster had noticed that, in an unguarded moment, the witness's hand had wandered to his side pocket, and was quickly withdrawn. Whereupon Mr. Webster sprang to his feet with the force of a giant, and with the voice of a lion exclaimed, "Out with it, sir!" and the affrighted witness drew from his pocket the testimony he had given, carefully written in the hand of the opposing counsel.

† Matt. xxvi. 24. Mark xiv. 21.

nunciations of God's word, and the deep convictions of their souls!

There is a kind of doom in the words "*that man;*" they dismiss the traitor. He is to be henceforth a stranger. "*That man,*" not a disciple. "That man," equivalent to "I know not whence thou art;" "Depart from me," "Worker of iniquity."

"It were good for that man if he had *never been born.*" But eternity is so long, and heaven is so glorious, that if a man should suffer a million ages, and then be restored, were it not better that he had been born? Yes, — if he could be restored.

This was no cant saying on the lips of Christ. He often spoke as if he knew that there is a fire which will never be quenched. Nor is this the language of rage; it is the announcement of one whose heart bleeds at being obliged to pronounce it. Our Lord was always calm when he spoke of retribution. His voice never trembled with uncertainty, and his vision was not limited, but his eye, undimmed, pierced both the glory and the gloom of endless ages. Who, after listening to his words, will dare face death unprepared?

Why falls not the traitor at the feet of the Master, imploring escape from such dreadful doom? Alas! how successfully Satan befools and befogs the mind that yields to him! How deaf the ear that heard not those terrible maledictions! There sat that insensible and guilty apostate unmoved, thinking of his bargain with the rulers, and of the coming opportunity to betray his Master, and of his suburban plot of ground, where he was to pass his future years, and fare sumptuously every day. "Thou *fool*, this night thy soul shall be required of thee."

John at length asked Christ plainly who it was that should betray him, for as yet no one knew save the betrayed and the betrayer. Jesus answered, "He it is to whom I shall give a sop, when I have dipped it." And when he had dipped the sop, when every eye was fixed, when every breath was hushed, when every heart had almost for the moment forgotten to beat, "he gave it to Judas Iscariot, the son of Simon," thereby fulfilling the Scripture, "If thine enemy hunger, feed him."

Then it was that Judas for the first time broke the silence, and with all the surprise of injured innocence inquired — what? "Is it I?" Our Saviour made a simple affirmative reply — "Thou hast said it." * John adds, "And after the sop, Satan entered into him." Then said Jesus, "What thou doest, do quickly. Now, no man at the table knew for what intent he spake this unto him. For some of them thought, because Judas had the bag, that Jesus had said unto him, Buy those things that we have need of against the feast; or, that he should give something to the poor. He then, having received the sop," glided out, like a serpent, into the darkness; "and it was night." † No wonder!

Judas had the effrontery, as he left, to take with him the treasures of the company; he had the money, the whole of it. He could now make his last payment for the land, if it had not already been paid for;

* Matt. xxvi. 25.

† John xiii. 26–30.

we suspect it had been; he was not the man to run much in debt; or he could now secure the adjoining lot — the ambition of every land-owner. But "what shall it profit a man if he shall gain the whole world, and lose his own soul?" The hour of mercy expired; the Holy Ghost withdrew; Satan triumphed; and a professor of religion, a preacher, an apostle, one of the twelve, completed the climax of iniquity; the deceiver, the hypocrite, the defaulter, and the traitor stands before us, possessed of the devil.

Be not startled. This is not an extinct species of madness. Now, as of yore, the devil possesses men. It is a proud record of the church, that its members are so largely prevented from falling into this condition, and from committing appalling crimes. The Knapps, Crowninshields, Greens, Websters, Evanses, and the like, were not professors of religion. Still, exceptions do appear. Deacon Samuel Andrews, the Kingston murderer, was an office-bearer in the church. Satan had worked much the same with him as with Judas. Andrews had for years tampered with vice. Hid in his house, concealed in his barn, buried in his cellar, were found various articles stolen from confiding neighbors. He had played the fatal game with his soul's enemy for small stakes, and had been permitted to win. He was then allured on to greater risks. He walked in the cemetery with Holmes. He had, before this, brooded over crime. He had more than once dallied with thoughts of murder. Holmes, at that time, had money about him; not much; only six hundred dollars. But Andrews's blood was hot. It had been heating for the deed.

There are twenty thousand more for him in the will. Why wait for natural death? Passion became master. A strange fire gleamed from his eyes, a stranger madness was enthroned in his heart. A stone at his feet was seized, a blow given, and all was over; for the devil had taken possession of his victim.

There are castles whose walls you partially descend by many steps. You reach a last one, followed, you naturally expect, by another, which you attempt to take; but a sheer, smooth wall plunges you instantly into a stepless and deadly abyss below. "After I threw the first stone, which stunned him," says Andrews, "I knew nothing more until I found myself washing my hands in the brook." Such is the plunge down the castle wall. Thus confessed Green. Not unlike this was Webster's confession. The fiend long lures us on, step by step; he watches for the ripened hour, and when it comes, he leaps to the will, and his murderous bidding is obeyed. Resistance at the first approach is necessary, or everything is jeopardized. Great crimes are always the outgrowth of minor ones, though, in their results and bearings, there are no minor crimes. The notorious criminal always thoroughly paves his pathway, and childhood often places the first stones. It is the preliminary tampering with sin that does the mischief. The journey of transgression is dangerous from the start. The man who yields, though in a thing often regarded unimportant, has stepped his foot upon a frightfully slippery place, and has taken a deadly serpent into his bosom.

Facts show how often the crime of Judas has been repeated, though under a great variety of circumstances. Men who have been intrusted with the money of others are tempted to appropriate some portion of it to their own use; it is to be thus employed only for a time; there is an honest intention of restoring it in full; it is a hard spot to bridge over; it is to help out from present difficulty some embarrassed friend; in the long run no one shall be wronged.* Cursed be such temptations! One had better go half clothed, half fed, and half starved; had better be the scorn of the more fashionable in community, rather than use, without the owner's consent or knowledge, one dollar or one farthing of his money. It is not so much the money, nor the use of the money; the amount taken may be so trifling that no crisis will result either way; but the amount cannot be so trifling that the character is not demoralized by the transaction. The man's self-respect receives thereby a deplorable shock. The key to the fortress is surrendered, and the devil will thereafter perplex and ruin the transgressor, if he can. A cunning, and a crafty, and a heartless wretch is Satan. Everything is allowed by him to go swimmingly prosperous for a

* It is not difficult to imagine that the preliminary defalcations of Judas were committed, not with reckless disregard of every consideration, but with much plausible reasoning. He may have only intended at first an investment for the corporation of which he was treasurer; or an investment for himself, with the intention of full restoration of the funds employed. Inability to do this, together with difficulty in meeting payments, may have led to continued thefts and false returns. At length, demoralized, and convinced of a speedy end to his Master's career, he was ripe for all the atrocities his history displayed.

time,* but he always deserts his victim when the rub comes; he helps into, but never out from difficulties, except to plunge one into still greater difficulties. He watches for the hour of ripening with keener eye than the husbandman watches his maturing crops; he knows when to assault his victim with multiplied temptations; he knows when to employ every recruit and every auxiliary; he knows how to hunt down and dog the guilty from place to place, until he extorts, if possible, unlimited compliance with his terms. As fire is a different thing when a servant upon the hearth and when lording it over our roof, so is Satan, when a suitor and when a tyrant.

> "Let no man trust the first false step of guilt;
> It hangs upon a precipice
> Whose steep descent in last perdition ends."

The progress, too, after one has fairly set out in a course of sin, increases with alarming augmentation. Thus, in the case of Judas, his cherished avariciousness was followed by unfaithfulness; then, in quick succession, by embezzlement, treachery, be-

* Psalm lxxiii.

There is a tree known as the *Judas tree*, which happily illustrates the deceitful and alluring character of sin. The blossoms appear before the leaves, and are of brilliant crimson. The flaming beauty of the flowers attracts innumerable insects, and the wandering bee is drawn to it to gather honey. But every bee that alights upon its blossoms imbibes a fatal opiate, and drops dead from among the crimson flowers to the earth. Beneath this enticing tree, the earth is strewn with the victims of its fatal fascinations.

trayal, and Satanic possession. The truth is, that every man has within him elements of eternal kinship, and also unexplored mines of wrath and death; that by which he may become little less than a God, on the one hand, or a baleful and everlasting wreck, upon the other. And mighty are the issues pending upon the start. There is no man of earnest soul, who does not, at times, actually feel himself trembling upon the appalling verge of remediless ruin; and a single step, at the critical moment, often results in the inevitable plunge.*

The fearful nature of crime, the startling capabilities of the human heart to commit crime, the treacherous beginnings and shocking terminations of crime, therefore appeal, as with the voice of God, to every one whose face is in the least turned towards any form of transgression, to escape at once from the impending doom. Emerson somewhere remarks that "man, though in brothels, or jails, or on gibbets, is on his way to all that is good and true." One important condition is herein overlooked — *everything depends upon which way the man's face is turned.*

Nay, the deep undertone of the whole universe is a solid entreaty to the sinful to repent and accept supernatural strength, for every one needs strength more than natural to pave the way through these perils of life up to a glorious immortality.

* Dr. South's statement of this thought is forcible: "There is no man breathing but carries about him a sleeping lion in his bosom, which God can and may, when he pleases, rouse up and let loose upon him, so as to tear and worry him, to that degree that he shall be glad to take sanctuary in a quiet grave."

A few hours only intervene after the last words of our Saviour, — "What thou doest, do quickly," — before new scenes crowd upon us. The lights are out in the supper-hall, the Master and his companions are among the cypress trees at the foot of the Mount of Olives, in the garden of Gethsemane. They are under the triple shadows of mountain, city, and ornamental trees. The traitor has, meantime, notified the rulers that everything is now in readiness. There are bustle and haste in the temple courts; this thing must be done by night, and before the common people get wind of the transaction; otherwise they will prevent it. The detachment guard of five hundred — the Roman cohort for the castle of Antonia — are ordered out. The captain of the temple, attended by the temple police, with a few private but interested citizens, together with the priests, rulers, and servants not on temple duty, are drawn up in line of march. Silently, at that midnight hour, headed by the captain, who was arm in arm with Judas, they thread their way through the streets of Jerusalem.* Judas is familiar

* The account, as gathered from the different evangelists, is the following: —

"When Jesus had spoken these words, he went forth with his disciples over the brook Cedron, where was a garden, into the which he entered, and his disciples. And Judas also, which betrayed him, knew the place; for Jesus ofttimes resorted thither with his disciples. Judas, then, having received a band of men and officers from the chief priests and Pharisees, cometh thither with lanterns, and torches, and weapons. Jesus, therefore, knowing all things that should come upon him, went forth, and said unto them, Whom seek ye? They answered him, Jesus of Nazareth. Jesus saith

with the way, and with all the private resorts of his Master, and knows the spot where he would this night be found; often had he visited it, in company with his Master. The troops now on the way are sufficient to surround it. This being silently done, their torches and lanterns are quickly lit, and their weapons drawn. Humanly speaking, escape is impossible. They approach gradually, drawing in towards the centre. The Master and the eleven are thereby exposed to full view.

"Now," says Matthew, "he that betrayed him gave them a sign, saying, Whomsoever I shall kiss,

unto them, I am he. And Judas also, which betrayed him, stood with them." John xviii. 1-5.

"And while he yet spake, lo, Judas, one of the twelve, came, and with him a great multitude, with swords and staves, from the chief priests and elders of the people. Now he that betrayed him gave them a sign, saying, Whomsoever I shall kiss, that same is he; hold him fast. And forthwith he came to Jesus, and said, Hail, Master; and kissed him. And Jesus said unto him, Friend, wherefore art thou come? Then came they, and laid hands on Jesus, and took him." Matt. xxvi. 47-50.

"And immediately, while he yet spake, cometh Judas, one of the twelve, and with him a great multitude, with swords and staves, from the chief priests, and the scribes, and the elders. And he that betrayed him had given them a token, saying, Whomsoever I shall kiss, that same is he; take him, and lead him away safely. And as soon as he was come, he goeth straightway to him, and saith, Master, Master; and kissed him." Mark xiv. 43-45.

"And while he yet spake, behold, a multitude, and he that was called Judas, one of the twelve, went before them, and drew near unto Jesus, to kiss him. But Jesus said unto him, Judas, betrayest thou the Son of man with a kiss?" Luke xxii. 47, 48.

that same is he; hold him fast." "Hold him fast." Mark the words! Ill at ease is Judas. "And," continues the narrative, "forthwith he came to Jesus, and said, Hail, Master; and kissed him." Horrors! Of a truth, the criminal capabilities of humanity are fiendish; that kiss, which should have remained as a world-wide and pure symbol of love, is henceforth an effaceless brand-mark upon the forehead of the race, indicative of lurking treachery and death.

"Companion," said our Lord, — such is the original, — "why standest thou here?" This question seemed to be the first syllable that stirred the conscience of Judas to due comprehension of his guilt.

Quickly followed another dreadful interrogation, which must have rolled like terrific thunder through the soul of the traitor — "Judas, betrayest thou the Son of man with a kiss?" For an instant their eyes met; beaming from the face of the one was calmness, mingled with mercy; stamped upon the face of the other was a rayless despair. The next instant, Jesus and his disciple separated, with a silent but eternal farewell.

It is well nigh the hour of morning. The temple seems quite deserted. The Levites are in the guard room. The priests on duty are within the court of the Israelites. All are suddenly startled by a heavy footfall, and panting breath, such as they are unused to hearing. Why comes this intruder here? But no guard is able to arrest him. See him, his eyes bloodshot, and in his outstretched hand is a bag of silver. He rushes past the Levite watch, under the vine-clad arch, into the sanctuary, into the court of the priests, even into the holy place (εν τω ναω), where no common Jew was allowed, and whence all Gentiles were interdicted, on penalty of death if they entered. But to this man the sanctity of the temple is nothing, the resentment of the priests is nothing; everything, save one thing, is as nothing. Give way! Stop him not! for a firebrand is in his bosom, and the avenger of blood is upon his track.

O wretched man! who shall deliver him? He tries to make restitution; as a last resource of his hopeless misery, he comes to the priests; God's ministers will surely pity him; he implores, and he begs, and he proffers the thirty pieces of silver, but they are like garments spotted with blood — nobody wants them. Alas for the thirty pieces of silver! Had they been talents of gold, they were no relief or atonement. His agony is every moment intensified; his conscience, which had suffered only an occasional twinge, now rises like an army with banners. "I have sinned, I have sinned," he exclaims, "in that I have betrayed *innocent* blood." "And they said, What is that to us? See thou to that." Heartless monsters! * Yes, they repel this ill-fated wretch;

* Often has this conduct been repeated. Young men have been admitted into the society of those who pass for gentlemen; they have lost everything upon the stake of a single throw, and being of no further service, have been spurned from the presence of those who but lately paid them every attention, and then have been kicked into the street, and told to go to the devil. That there is honor among thieves, and the like, is, oftener than otherwise, merely a myth.

they gibe him with heartless language; they heed not the remorse-stung victim whom, but shortly before, they had embraced; they see his distress, but they had used him as long as they wanted anything of him, and now they bid him begone. "It is none of our business; away, thou fool."

The horror-stricken man deigns not a word in reply; at the feet of the astonished priests he flings the accursed blood-money; the chink of it, sounding like a death-knell, seems to startle anew the betrayer; he flies to find rest in solitude, but fails in his search; he dares stay on earth no longer, and he will *feel*, rather than longer *fear*, the torments of the lost.

He speeds onward, past the palace of Herod, away from the tower of Antonia, in the opposite direction from the garden of Gethsemane; no course is more natural, and none more fatal; onward, onward like a madman he rushes; he thinks that they who loved Jesus are about to kill him; like Cain, he feels that every man's hand is against him; that his punishment is greater than he can bear. His dejection becomes despair; the pains of hell get hold upon him; Satan tantalizes him, and aggravates every sin and mistake of his life; the purity of Christ's life haunts and condemns him. "*Innocent* blood!" "innocent *blood!*" is before his eyes, and stains his hands. Had it been sinful blood, he could have washed it off; tranquillized would have been his despair if one false step in that faultless life of Christ could have been recalled. "Blood, blood!" exclaimed Booth, the murderer of Lincoln. Indelible ever are the stains of innocent blood; the waters of the "multitudinous seas" cannot wash them off.* Murder will out! No nook nor corner in the whole universe of God can conceal a murderer.† No sooner does the horrified Judas plant his feet for the last time upon his intended future homestead, that charming spot purchased by money stolen from poor people and the bag, than he feels that every finger in Jerusalem is pointing him out, and that every voice, loaded with a curse, pronounces him *thief*, *traitor*, and *murderer!* He tries to reason with himself: "I have done no murder; the priests are the ones who are killing Jesus; and yet—I am an accomplice; nay, the principal. 'Tis my hand that struck the blow, my spear ran him through. Can I not pray?

> 'What if this cursed hand
> Were thicker than itself with brothers' blood?
> Is there not rain enough in the sweet heavens
> To wash it white as snow?
> Try what repentance can. What can it not?
> Yet what can it, when one cannot repent?
> O wretched state! O bosom black as death!
> O limed soul!'‡

What, is there no security here? Am I not upon my own soil?" Your own soil! That charming plot of ground has become the most frightful spot on God's earth.

See! The eyes of the betrayer start from their sockets, his lips are pallid, he trembles like a scourged

* Shakespeare.

† Daniel Webster's plea at the trial of the Knapps for the murder of Captain White. See Appendix H.

‡ Hamlet.

slave; on every hand he hears the groans of dying men; the rustling leaf is the breath of an enemy, and every sound is an avenger's footfall. All things mean mischief; every grape-vine conceals a dagger, poised and trembling to leap into his heart; every nook is crowded with murderers.

> "Have mercy, Jesu! Soft; I did but dream.
> O, coward conscience, how dost thou afflict me!
> The lights burn blue. It is now dead midnight.
> Cold, fearful drops stand on my trembling flesh.
> What do I fear? Myself? There's none else by:
> . . . .
> Is there a murderer here? No; yes; I am.
> Then fly. What, from myself? Great reason; why?
> Lest I revenge. What? Myself on myself?
> I love myself. Wherefore? For any good
> That I myself have done unto myself?
> O, no; alas, I rather hate myself
> For hateful deeds committed by myself.
> I am a villain; yet I lie, I am not.
> Fool, of thyself speak well. Fool, do not flatter.
> My conscience hath a thousand several tongues,
> And every tongue brings in a several tale,
> And every tale condemns me for a villain.
> Perjury, perjury, in the high'st degree,
> All several sins, all used in each degree,
> Throng to the bar, crying all, Guilty, guilty!
> I shall despair. There is no creature loves me;
> And, if I die, no soul will pity me:
> Nay, wherefore should they? since that I myself
> Find in myself no pity to myself.*

Unfortunate and wretched man, did you think on that spot of ground to build a royal home? Did you

* Richard III.

expect to hold some official position among your fellow-citizens? Did you imagine that the noted men of the realm would visit you, and sup at your table, and praise your vines and wines? Did you intend there to pass your years with a queenly wife, and with happy children? How overwhelming the defeat you have met!

> "Seeing that face, I could but fear the end;
> For death was in it, looking through his eyes,
> Nor could I follow, to arrest the fate,
> That drove him madly on with scorpion whip."

Does the eye of any one who is securing property by gains and means which are questionable, fall upon this page? Is he fancying that the day will come when he can retire from the turmoil of business, and enjoy his ill-gotten possessions? God's providence, and an experience well nigh universal, thunder, "No, he shall not." There is less happiness for him than for the honest savage in his jungle home.

What makes voluntary suicide at once detestable and horrifying, is its embodiment of rebellion against God, and a defiant forth-stepping to his judgment bar. It is the natural expression of extreme self-condemnation, and also a type of eternal condemnation. It is not always the worst step in a man's life, but it points back to a terrible declension in the way to ruin.

From this frightful condition in which Judas found himself, he at once completed his resolve to rush to perdition. Every facility was at hand. The most probable facts are the following:* An overhanging limb of a tree, growing upon the edge of the declivity, was selected; the strap which for three years had held the money bag was attached to the limb, and then adjusted about the neck; a single bound, and the victim dangled for a moment in the air; the well-worn strap snapped asunder; the tree shook off the self-murderer; his own soil spurned him; he was hurled from one jagged point to another; the strangled

* The statements made are based upon the following Scripture data: —

"Then Judas, which had betrayed him, when he saw that he was condemned, repented himself, and brought again the thirty pieces of silver to the chief priests and elders, saying, I have sinned in that I have betrayed the innocent blood. And they said, What is that to us? See thou to that. And he cast down the pieces of silver in the temple, and departed, and went and hanged himself." Matt. xxvii. 3-5.

"Now this man purchased a field with the reward of iniquity; and falling headlong, he burst asunder in the midst, and all his bowels gushed out. And it was known unto all the dwellers at Jerusalem; insomuch as that field is called, in their proper tongue, Aceldama, that is to say, The field of blood." Acts i. 18, 19.

Story's description of the discovery of the corpse is graphic: —

"The sky was dark with heavy, lowering clouds;
A lifeless, stifling air weighed on the world;
A dreadful silence like a nightmare lay
Crouched on its bosom, waiting, grim and gray,
In horrible suspense of some dread thing.
A creeping sense of death, a sickening smell,
Infected the dull breathing of the wind.
A thrill of ghosts went by me now and then,

wretch burst asunder in his descent; and we turn to hide our eyes from the mangled and disgusting corpse that lies below in the dark ravine, over which the evangelist has thrown a friendly mantle, in which are inwrought these simple but impressive words: "*Gone to his own place.*" That mantle we will not attempt to lift, but may be permitted to add to the epitaph one word — DEFEATED.

And made my flesh creep as I wandered on.
At last I came to where a cedar stretched
Its black arms out beneath a dusky rock,
And, passing through its shadow, all at once
I started; for against the dubious light
A dark and heavy mass, that to and fro
Swung slowly with its weight, before me grew.
A sick, dread sense came over me; I stopped —
I could not stir. A cold and clammy sweat
Oozed out all over me; and all my limbs,
Bending with tremulous weakness like a child's,
Gave way beneath me. Then a sense of shame
Aroused me. I advanced, stretched forth my hand,
And pushed the shapeless mass; and at my touch
It yielding swung — the branch above it creaked,
And back returning, struck against my face.
A human body! Was it dead, or not?
Swiftly my sword I drew, and cut it down,
And on the sand all heavily it dropped.
I plucked the robes away, exposed the face —
'Twas Judas, as I feared, cold, stiff, and dead:
That suffering heart of his had ceased to beat."

THE TRIUMPH.

Until the grave, the rod and cross will lie on us; but then comes their end. PAUL GERHARDT.

Providence has a wild, rough, incalculable road to its end, and it is of no use to try to whitewash its huge, mixed instrumentalities, or to dress up that terrific benefactor in a clean shirt and white neck-cloth of a student in divinity.

EMERSON.

The eternal stars shine out as soon as it is dark enough.

CARLYLE.

When sorrows come, they come not single spies, but in battalions. SHAKESPEARE.

Extraordinary afflictions are not always the punishment of extraordinary sins, but sometimes the trial of extraordinary graces. MATTHEW HENRY.

Affliction is a school or academy, wherein the best scholars are prepared for the commencement days of the Deity.

ROBERT BURTON.

A virtuous and well-disposed person is like good metal, — the more he is fired the more he is fined; the more he is opposed, the more he is approved. Wrongs may well try him, and touch him, but they cannot imprint on him any false stamp. RICHELIEU.

I consider how a man comes out of the furnace; gold will lie for a month in the furnace without losing a grain.

CECIL.

Times of general calamity and confusion have ever been productive of the greatest minds. The purest ore is produced from the hottest furnace, and the brightest thunderbolt is elicited from the darkest storm. COLTON.

Trial brings man face to face with God; the flimsy veil of bright cloud is blown away; he feels that he is standing outside the earth, with nothing between him and the Eternal Infinite. O, there is something in the sick bed, and the restlessness and the languor of shattered health, and the sorrow of affections withered, and the stream of life poisoned at the fountain, and the cold, lonely feeling of utter sadness of the heart, — what is felt when God strikes home in earnest, — that forces a man to feel what is real and what is not.

ROBERTSON.

Only one moment of weakness, think you? — one single moment more; . . . but *that* moment is the one selected by the tempter for a last trial, and in it you are about to ruin his hopes forever, or to give them fresh vigor. Courage, then! Stand firm! Give not back a single step! Falter not for a moment! Dispel every illusion of the enemy! Prove to him that with you he loses both his time and his trouble. And, by the reception which you give him, compel him to recognize in the *disciple* the Master who overcame him in the wilderness. MONOD.

What claim can that man have to courage who trembles at the frowns of fortune? True heroism consists in being superior to the ills of life, in whatever shape they may challenge you to combat. NAPOLEON.

THE TRIUMPH.

EACH man's life is both a fact and a symbol. Everybody has, therefore, both a real and a typical history. The actual and the typical history of Judas are before us; he is found to be a type of defeated humanity in all ages. Mankind, likewise, has other phases of character, and special representatives of the same.

The opposite of defeat is triumph. No one can fail of calling to mind one of the grandest types of triumphant conflict which history records, and every reader will justify careful analysis and application.

While Abraham was living in Uz of the Chaldees, amid scenes of idolatry, while Greece was scarcely more than a frontier settlement, — such as the New England coast appeared upon the arrival of the Pilgrims, — and while Melchisedek, a noble priest and prince, was ruling the charming region of Salem, had we passed down the eastern slope of the mountains separating Palestine from Arabia, we should have traversed estates belonging to a man who was no less faithful than Abraham, no less a Christ-like prince than Melchisedek, and who, taken all in all, is one of the noblest and most faultless characters recorded in history. This man bears the name of Job.*

Most modern scholars of note, it is well known, whether sceptical or orthodox, agree that the Book of Job, which records the trials of this patriarch, is one of the most ancient as well as one of the most sublime masterpieces among literary productions.†

Some there are, it is true, who have, in times past, looked upon Job, not as a real, but as a fictitious character; still it is equally true that at the present time there exists comparatively little doubt that Job is the name of a real person, whose essential history is recorded in the book bearing his name, and that he is as really a person, as David, Paul, and Martin Luther are real and not fictitious characters. The

* Appendix I.

† "I call our *Book of Job*, apart from all theories about it," says Carlyle, "one of the grandest things ever written with pen. One feels, indeed, as if it were not Hebrew; such a noble universality, different from noble patriotism or sectarianism, reigns in it. A noble book; all men's book! It is our first, oldest statement of the never-ending problem, man's destiny, and God's ways with him here on this earth. And all in such free flowing; grand in its sincerity, in its complicity, in its epic melody, and repose of reconcilement. There is the seeing eye, the mildly understanding heart. So *true*, every way; true eyesight and vision for all things; material things no less than spiritual; the horse, 'hast thou clothed his neck with *thunder?* — he *laughs* at the shaking of the spear!' Such living likenesses were never seen drawn. Sublime sorrow, sublime reconciliation; oldest choral melody as of the heart of mankind; so soft and great; as the summer midnight, as the world with its seas and stars! There is nothing written, I think, in the Bible or out of it, of equal literary merit."

freedom of all early Hebrew writings from such like fictions; the reference to Job, as an actual personage, in other and later parts of the Bible; the numerous traditions in the East respecting the patriarch and his family;* the improbability that a Hebrew would have invented a character so faultless, yet not belonging to his own race; the remarkable consistency in the development of the various characters introduced; and the singular air of truthfulness pervading the entire narrative, — contain a mass of accumulative evidence absolutely unanswerable, in favor of the reality of Job's existence and history. Entertaining these opinions, we

* The following scriptural references establish the fact of the high estimate placed upon Job, and likewise the reality of his existence: —

"The word of the Lord came again to me, saying, Son of man, when the land sinneth against me by trespassing grievously, then will I stretch out mine hand upon it, and will break the staff of the bread thereof and will send famine upon it, and will cut off man and beast from it. Though these three men, Noah, Daniel, and Job, were in it, they should deliver but their own souls by their righteousness, saith the Lord God." Ezekiel xiv. 12–14.

"Behold, we count them happy which endure. Ye have heard of the patience of Job, and have seen the end of the Lord; that the Lord is very pitiful, and of tender mercy." James v. 11.

Traditions found in the *Koran*, also in D'Herbelot's *Bibl. Orient*, establish, beyond controversy, the fact that there was such a person as Job, who lived in the patriarchal age, and who, above all other men, was distinguished for his sufferings and his patience. Throughout Arabia, reverence for the name of Job has been very great, and continues thus to the present day. The noblest families claim that they are descended from this patriarch.

shall be the better prepared to review the life of Job, and gather therefrom some of the more important and representative lessons.

Of his early life we have no data save those based upon questionable tradition.* We are, at the outset, introduced to a man whose wealth, consisting in part of rich and extensive lands, and in part of multitudes of flocks, was immense. Relatively, but few men, in modern times, would outrate him. In addition to this, his domestic relations seem to have been correspondingly felicitous; his family was numerous and prosperous. He was, likewise, a man of refinement and culture, — refinement and culture, we mean, in the truest and broadest sense of these terms. His lands lay upon the great thoroughfares of merchants who passed between Temah, Sheba, and Egypt. He thereby had abundant and favorable opportunities for collecting all the varied information then known to the world; of this he seems to have been master. The lofty tone pervading the speeches of Job shows that he was a sage, compared with which many in present times, who pretend much, but know little, are

* Job, or Aiub, is reported by some of the Arabian historians to have been descended from Ishmael: by others, his descent is traced from Isaac, through Esau, from whom he was the third, or at most the fourth in succession. And in the history given by Khendemír, who distinguishes him by the title of *The Patient*, it is stated that by his mother's side he was descended from Lot; that he had been commissioned by God to preach the faith to a people of Syria; that although no more than three had been converted by his preaching, he was, notwithstanding, rewarded for his zeal by immense possessions, &c.

as dust in the balance. In fact, there is a solemnity, a solidity, a majesty and grandeur, in this Arabian hero, compared with which the frothiness of modern cant and mannerism shows in the most pitiable contrast.*

In addition to all this, Job was a man of high political rank; he was a prince, alike successful in war and prosperous in peace. "He was the greatest of all the men in the East," says the Arabian proverb.†

* Hengstenberg is right in his conclusion that for depth of religious knowledge Job stands even higher than Abraham.

† This agrees with his description of himself. The translation we follow throughout the discussion is that by Thomas Wemyss.

"Then Job continued his discourse, and said,
'O that it were with me as in months that are past,
In the days when God was my guardian!
When his lamp shone over my head,
And by his light I walked through darkness:
As I was when in the prime of my life,
When God guarded my tabernacle:
When my vigor was still in me,
And my family were round about me:
When streams of milk flowed where I went,
And the rock poured me out rivers of oil:
When I walked early through the city,
And a seat was set for me in the streets.
The young men saw me and made way for me;
The aged ranged themselves around me.
The rulers restrained themselves from talking,
And laid their hand upon their mouth.
The nobles observed silence,
Their tongue cleaved to the roof of their mouth.
When the ear heard me it blessed me;
When the eye saw me it gave signs of approbation;

United with all this was a reputation he had gained which was worth more than his money, his flocks, his merchandise, and his princely authority. He was known, far and near, as a man of faultless integrity. He was pronounced by the Lord himself as "a perfect and an upright man, one that feareth God and escheweth evil."

For I delivered the poor when they implored assistance,
And the orphan who had no defender.
The blessing of him who was perishing came upon me,
And I caused the widow's heart to sing for joy.
I put on equity, and clothed myself with it;
My justice was as a robe and a diadem.
I was eyes to the blind,
I was feet to the lame;
I was a father to the destitute,
And I inquired carefully into the cause of the stranger.
I broke the jaws of the wicked,
And plucked the prey out of his teeth.
Then I said, I shall die in my nest,
I shall multiply my days as the palm tree;
My root shall spread out to the waters;
The dew of night shall repose on my branches;
My glory shall be unfading around me,
And my bow continue fresh in my hand.'
" 'To me men gave ear and attended;
They were silent at my admonition.
After I had spoken they replied not,
For my reasons dropped on them as dew.
They waited for me as for a spring shower;
They opened wide their mouths, as for the harvest-rain.
If I smiled on them, they were gay,
And rejoiced in my benignant aspect;
If I frequented their society, I sat as a chief;
I dwelt as a king among warriors,
As one who comforteth the mourners.' " (Chap. xxix.)

In a word, his was a life of unalloyed prosperity, faultless piety, and unquestioned rectitude: he was honored of men and approved of God.

In the further development of the narrative, strange as it may seem, we are admitted for a moment behind the veil which conceals the ordinarily hidden arrangements and assignments of Providence, and are permitted to look in upon the private council-chamber of Jehovah, and to see for once what things are sometimes said and done therein. Typical as well as actual is this entire drama, and every man is, more or less, first or last, enrolled to play some part.*

The divine nature, and the evil nature, and human nature, are much the same to-day they were four thousand years ago. Temptations come to every heart in some form, and gigantic, though unestimated, are the issues pending.

One entered that council-chamber, of whom the Lord inquired if he had seen, in his wanderings, that model of human excellence in the person of the Arabian Job.† He said he had, but added, in terms of

* Other passages speak of the privy council of the Most High. Job xv. 8. Ps. lxxxix. 7. Jer. xxiii. 18. 1 Kings xxii. 19. Dan. vii. 9, 10.

† The presence of Satan in heaven may at first glance appear surprising, but not upon second thought. For if pre-existent humanity, in which the Logos embodied itself long before coming to earth (John vi. 62; iii. 13; xvii. 5), was a higher type of creation than the angels, and if Satan was of the highest order of angelic creation, then, when pre-existing humanity came into being and was placed upon the throne, there was an occasion for the origin of pride, jealousy, and rebellion on the part of Satan. And when the command

low insinuation, that this Job was serving God only upon the ground of some selfish policy. Job does not

was given, "Let all the angels of God worship him" (Heb. i. 6), the spirit of rebellion might manifest itself in open revolt. His prestige was gone. He should have submitted to God's will, but did not; he rebelled.

Of the fact of this rebellion there can be no question. (Rev. xii. 7.) The thought of war in heaven seems not quite compatible with the consistency of things. But wars have just as much right in a probationary heaven as on the earth; they have no right anywhere. An enlarged view of things will find not much inconsistency in having the proud and ambitious wars of earth prefigured by those of the spiritual world ages past. Also, when historic humanity was created in the person of Adam, there was another occasion for the further exercise of jealousy and malignity on the part of Satan and his minions. But probably he did not, at that time, descend to the lowest degradation, or possibly below recovery. He had lost rank by his first transgression, but not to such extent as to exclude him from heaven. He was held in respect by the angels. (Jude 9.) It will, doubtless, some time be revealed, that God has been merciful to the fallen angels as well as to fallen humanity. May not Satan have been left for a time upon probation? May not the opportunity for repentance given him have been like that given to mortals? There were elect (1 Tim. v. 21), why not non-elect angels? In this connection, "the Lamb slain from the foundation of the world" is significant. (Rev. xiii. 8.)

But when the historic God-man appeared, then the old spirit of rebellion, which first showed itself in heaven against the pre-existent spiritual God-man, rose to its height, and in that mad and reckless endeavor to tempt and destroy the Son of God (Matt. iv. 1–12), Satan forfeited all claims to mercy, and did irreparable damage to his moral character. That was an act of blasphemy. He then committed, as it seems to us, the unpardonable sin, and fell, as lightning, from

serve God for nought, is the charge. It is profit Job is after. It is profit all your supposed good men are after. There is no reverence for God in all their show of piety. "You have blessed Job," Satan seems to say, "and he does well to serve you. Who would not? But it is merely hypocrisy. Job is saying, 'Lord! Lord!' while his heart is far from thee. Strip him now of his splendid round of prosperity with which you have hedged him in; touch his money, then see if he cares for thee. He will no longer serve thee; he will mock thee and curse thee to thy face."

It is not a little surprising that Jehovah allowed such insolence in his presence; but then we know he permitted similar real or apparent insults, twenty centuries later, in the wilderness.* On the judgment day it will be wise for the Judge to have a clear case against Satan. When we better know the purpose which all present transactions are to subserve in the universe, we can much better answer the many perplexing questions which almost daily confront us.† It

heaven (Luke x. 18), never again to enter it. The heavens could well rejoice; the accuser had gone from their midst (Rev. xii. 10); and the earth might wail for the woe that his abiding presence brought upon it. (Rev. xii. 12.) He was left, henceforth, until the end at least, to fill his cup brim full of iniquity, in preparation for his final banishment into perdition. See *Outlines of Christian Theology*, by the Author.

* Matt. iv. 3–10. Luke iv. 1–13.

† Hengstenberg makes a good note upon this thought. "The question put by a savage, 'Why, then, does not God strike Satan dead?' could only have been retailed as apparently ingenious, by men who stood spiritually on a level with the savages. Satan is a very important element in the

was this misrepresentation on the part of Satan which called forth from Jehovah the following language: "And the Lord said unto Satan, Behold, all that he hath is in thy power; only upon himself put not forth thine hand. So Satan went forth from the presence of the Lord," — and the sun went down at high noon.

While Job was in the height of his prosperity, while his sons and his daughters, according to an Eastern custom, were feasting at the elder brother's house, while the oxen were ploughing in the field, while the flocks were pasturing on the hill-side, and while the camels were *en route* with this prosperous man's merchandise, — everything was changed in a day. So has it been, so is it, and so will it be again. Tears often flood the face almost before the smile of the last moment has gone, and we hear sobs almost before the echo of the laugh dies out from the adjacent hall.

Why hastens that servant of Job across the fields? Admit him! "Sir!" is his salutation. "Say on," is the reply. "The oxen were ploughing, and the asses feeding beside them, and the Sabeans fell upon them, and took them away; yea, they have slain the servants with the edge of the sword; and I only am escaped alone to tell thee."

Hard times are these for a good man, with no reason this side of heaven assigned for it. This vast source of income cut off in a moment, must make even a

divine economy. God needs him, and he therefore keeps him until he shall have no more use for him. Then will he be banished to his own place. The Scriptures call the wicked heathen tyrant Nebuchadnezzar a servant of God. They might give Satan the same name."

rich man feel poor. The opulent prince is less rich than he was at daybreak.

But why hastens homeward this other servant, even before the first had ceased speaking? Have the oxen and the flocks been recaptured from those lawless freebooters?

"Sir," is the salutation; "Say on," the reply.

"The fire of God is fallen from heaven, and hath burned up the sheep, and the servants, and consumed them; and I only am escaped alone to tell thee."

Surely evils never come single-handed. When it rains this kind of rain, it pours. It is ruin, not loss, which now glares into the face and eyes of the patriarch.

But he has something left, and it is a long road that has no turn in it. The next servant will surely bring better tidings.

Listen! "While the last was yet speaking," we read, "there came also another, and said, The Chaldeans made out three bands, and fell upon the camels, and have carried them away, yea, and slain the servants with the edge of the sword; and I only am escaped alone to tell thee."

Fearful is this accumulation of ills! Darker and thicker comes the night apace. He is land-poor; having land, but no use for it. God pity the man who is rich and poor the same day; who is full, at ease, one day, but filled with trouble the next; who looks through golden avenues to-day, but to-morrow looks through avenues of red hot coals or gray ashes, or, what is worse, sees nought save a heaven and earth draped in weeds of mourning. It is the suddenness and the painful precision of such like things which give the shock. A single misfortune may come, as accident (some think), or in the natural order of events (as others infer), but this, blow on blow, swift, sudden, terrible, and, in such graduated climax, anguish upon anguish, this smiting a man when he is down, — there is no accident in this; intelligence, — malignant or otherwise, — intelligence is the moving hand; designed visitations are there, and nothing other.*

* Kitto makes the following note upon Satan's method in Job's afflictions: —

"The apostle assumes that we are not ignorant of Satan's devices (2 Cor. ii. 11), and among the sources of our knowledge respecting them, the history of Job and his trials is most conspicuous. An attentive consideration of the whole matter, in that point of view, would be most instructive. To track his various windings, dodges, and manœuvres for the purpose of circumventing Job, and of bringing peril upon his soul, might be made a study of surpassing interest and high edification. Look, for instance, at his penetrating knowledge of man's heart, and his masterly generalship in working upon it, as evinced in the mere ardor and succession of his assaults upon Job. After having, as he supposed, weakened and dispirited this good man by his previous attacks, he came with his most fierce and terrible charge last of all, confident that by this management the last stroke must overwhelm and destroy him. This seems to be a favorite tactic with him, to come down upon us with his strongest assaults when he thinks we are the weakest. It is easy to perceive that if Satan had suffered Job to hear first of the death of his children, all the rest would have been of small account to him. Little would he have cared for the loss of his cattle *after* having heard that all his children had been crushed to death by the fall of the house. As when some one great sorrow falls upon us, the heart can find no joy in the good that

But still a man will endure many and severe losses in temporal things, bite his trembling lip, hold back his tears, force a smile, and stand erect, provided that he still has a happy and unbroken family circle to go to. It is the good home which affords the best *anchorage* in storm time. Many a man has returned at nightfall, property gone, business disastrous; but kneeling in prayer, he said, "Thank God, my wife and children are spared me." And he has encouraged them, and said, "Though we shall be a little pinched, still together we can build up again."

Job's family was up to this time untouched; he could bear much else and much more; although that night would look upon a poor man, stripped of vast wealth, still he could sleep, for his children, of whom he was justly proud, were spared.

But, what! another messenger of ill! It cannot be; and yet, when things are going amiss, it seems as though there is no end or let up. "While the last was yet speaking," continues the narrative, "there came also another, and said, Thy sons and thy daughters

at other times bestows delight, so also does one great evil swallow up all sense and feeling of lesser troubles. Here, therefore, we behold the wiliness of Satan. Lest Job should lose any of the smart of the lesser afflictions, lest they should all have been swallowed up in the greater, he lays them out in order, the lesser first, the greater last, that his victims may not lose one drop of the bitterness in the cup mixed by the lord of poisons for him. It reminds one of the continental executions of great criminals in the last age, when the condemned was tortured, maimed, and broken before the *coup de grace* was given. Had this stroke been given at first, all else had been nothing."

were eating and drinking wine in their eldest brother's house: and behold there came a great wind from the wilderness, and smote the four corners of the house, and it fell upon the young men, and they are dead; and I only am escaped alone to tell thee."

Horrors and madness! Who can believe that God takes care of his children after this? Welcome atheism and infidelity! Why not? What good does it do to serve God and be honest, if such are the returns? Who makes money in this world? — none but good men? Nay, verily! We should not wonder much if the godless man will make just as much money as the godly man, and hold it just as long.

See this good man, stripped of property, bereft of children, blighted, ruined! Shall he still believe in God? Will he not curse God and die? Hush! and hear what one of God's heroes can say: "Then Job arose, and rent his mantle, and shaved his head, and fell down upon the ground, and worshipped, and said, Naked came I out of my mother's womb, and naked shall I return thither: The Lord gave, and the Lord hath taken away; blessed be the name of the Lord."

The sublimest words of resignation that ever fell from the lips of mortal are these. And more than this, they announce to the world that the devil is conquered at the hands of a *man*. Satan had thoroughly planned his campaign; he had things pretty much his own way; he made the onslaught with every advantage in his favor, but he met his match, received the worst hurt possible, and then retreated from the field, to try, if permitted, again.

Returning once more to the narrative, we read,

"Again there was a day when the sons of God came to present themselves before the Lord, and Satan came also among them to present himself before the Lord. And the Lord said unto Satan, From whence comest thou? And Satan answered the Lord, and said, From going to and fro in the earth, and from walking up and down in it. And the Lord said unto Satan, Hast thou considered my servant Job, that there is none like him in the earth, a perfect and an upright man, one that feareth God and escheweth evil? and still he holdeth fast his integrity, although thou movedst me against him, to destroy him without cause. And Satan answered the Lord, and said, Skin for skin, yea, all that a man hath will he give for his life. But put forth thy hand now, and touch his bone and his flesh, and he will curse thee to thy face. And the Lord said unto Satan, Behold, he is in thy hand; but save his life." *

A man may suffer much loss, yet if he has his health, he can recover much. Sound health is worth a fortune; at least, many a man, who has it not, thinks so.

But it turns out that he who had suffered enough to ruin most men was overtaken by a disease, the worst then or since known to mortals. It was a terrible type of the black leprosy of Syria. The appalling character of this malady is such as almost to preclude its description. It is a burning ulceration, covering the entire body. The hair falls off, the beard drops out, the eyelashes are lost, the eyes remain open

* Job ii. 1-6.

and fixed, the palms of the hands and soles of the feet swell out, and friends are compelled to fly from the sight of the victim. The mind of the sufferer is afforded only odd moments of sleep; frightful dreams, despondency, and despair prompting to self-murder, are some of the attending symptoms.

Satan's permission to attack the person of Job has resulted as we should expect. He selected the worst disease known, and wrought out its worst type. How much like the devil is such a course! If a man falls into the hands of Satan, he may depend upon one thing at least — he will do his worst by him.

Job's description of himself is graphic. "My flesh is clothed with worms and clods of dust, my skin is broken and become loathsome, and on my eyelids is the shadow of death. My bones are pierced in me in the night season, and my sinews take no rest. By the great force of my disease, my garments are changed. My skin is black upon me, and my bones are burned with heat. I am a brother to dragons and a companion of owls. They that are younger than I have me in derision, whose fathers I would have disdained to have set with the dogs of my flock. They were viler than the earth. And now I am their song; yea, I am their by-word. They abhor me, they flee from me, and spare not to spit in my face. My acquaintance are verily estranged from me. My kinsfolk have failed, and my familiar friends have forgotten me. They that dwell in my house, and my maids, count me for a stranger. I am an alien in their sight. I called my servant, and he gave me no answer; I entreated him with my mouth. My breath is strange to my wife, though I entreated for the children's sake of mine own body. Yea, young children despised me; I arose, and they spake against me. All my inward friends abhorred me; and they whom I loved are turned against me. My bone cleaveth to my skin and to my flesh, and I am escaped with the skin of my teeth. Have pity upon me, have pity upon me, O ye my friends, for the hand of God hath touched me." *

Poor man, we pity thee, and would help thee if we could; strange is it that God does not!

At this critical point in the narrative, a new character is introduced — Job's wife. It seems strange that Satan had not destroyed her with the children; but perhaps he had some design in not doing so. He may have thought to use this woman as an instrument in accomplishing his ultimate purposes. He hoped, no doubt, that she would prove another Eve.

It is possible that more than one very good man has had a very bad wife; but that proves nothing in the present instance. Job's wife, we think, ought not to be blamed overmuch.† She showed some weakness in those seasons of affliction, and who would not?

Look charitably at the case for a moment. The losses, we must bear in mind, were hers, as well as his. The property was gone; the manly eldest born, and the tender younger born, had fallen; and her husband was almost worse than dead. These griefs

* For fuller description consult Job ii. 7, 8; iii. 23–26; vi. 8–10; vii. 4, 5, 13–16; xix. 16–21; xxx. 17–31.

† Spanheim calls Job's wife a second Xantippe. J. D. Michaelis thinks she was spared to Job to complete the measure of his misfortune.

and calamities were hers to bear, as well as his. The woman was bewildered, and no wonder. Will not a wife sometimes allow her own name to be slandered, rather than suffer her husband to bear reproach?

Stripped of his fortune, his children, for whom he had never forgotten to offer God a morning sacrifice, buried amid the ruins of their own dwelling, which the fierce tornado had levelled to the ground, "the best man in the world becoming the most miserable man in the world," presents a gloomy enough picture. His wife felt this. Can we blame her that the cloud of infidelity dimmed her eyesight for a moment?

Ay, who is the Almighty, that one should serve him, or what profit is there if we pray unto him? Do not the words almost rise to our own lips, as they must have weighed upon her consciousness? Could this series of evils happen without the will and pleasure of God? Could not he have prevented them? Would not the woman almost escape our condemnation, should she be left to say, What does integrity amount to? Does righteousness protect a man against life's ills? Why does it not protect you, my husband? They lie who say your life is not next to perfect. You are a just and perfect man. If God lives, and loves goodness and integrity better than vice and iniquity, why steps he not forth to your rescue? There is no God save Fate; and Fate is no God.

It was this overwhelming pressure upon the afflicted woman which left her crushed-hearted, and which well nigh drove her on to madness. Her advice was terrible, but it does not prove that she was a *shrew*. Satan seems to have taken possession for a moment, and prompted her to tempt Job with the very words he had predicted Job would employ when afflicted. "He will curse thee to thy face," said Satan. "Curse God and die," said his wife.*

Job, do you hear! The universe listens to catch your answer. It breathlessly awaits the vital issue pending. You are a spectacle for the angels to look at. God's credit is staked upon what you say and do.

Smarting under his accumulation of woes, his soul wrung with anguish, his face haggard with frightful anxiety, and ghastly under a wasting disease, pale, trembling, and almost hideous, he rose, rent his mantle, and replied to his wife's temptation, — "Shall we receive good at the hand of God, and shall we not receive evil?"

Splendid, thou earth-born giant! A gala day was that in heaven. The sons of God everywhere shouted for joy over the moral grandeur of this conquest. It was proved, on that day, that goodness can exist in this world, — the devil to the contrary, notwithstanding, — irrespective of earthly reward, and that man can fear and love God, when every inducement to selfishness is taken away. That is a victory, such, doubtless, as God would have every one achieve.

The narrative next brings to our notice other char-

* There seems to be some little confusion resulting from the different translations of the word *barach;* "to bless" and "to curse" are both given by commentators. The present connection demands the latter, though usage perhaps equally justifies the former rendering. It involves, probably, in either case, a kind of parting salutation, as if she had said, God can do nothing for you. Bid him a farewell that will last forever.

acters — the personal friends of Job. Their introduction to us is very beautiful. There is in it a kind of poetic and majestic tenderness.

"Now, when Job's three friends heard of all this evil that was come upon him, they came every one from his own place; Eliphaz the Temanite, and Bildad the Shuhite, and Zophar the Naamathite: for they had made an appointment together to come to mourn with him and to comfort him. And when they lifted up their eyes afar off, and knew him not, they lifted up their voice, and wept; and they rent every one his mantle, and sprinkled dust upon their heads toward heaven. So they sat down with him upon the ground, seven days and seven nights, and none spake a word unto him: for they saw that his grief was very great." *

Silence is indeed much better sometimes than spoken consolation. Job's friends were wise, knowing this fact, to act in the present instance accordingly. But their countenances, nevertheless, were expressive, and spoke a kind of language well known to Job. Often this language of the face is by far the loudest.

Day after day, these princes and friends of Job kept more or less near the afflicted man, and at such times as the taking of food, rest, and sleep allowed, they continued revolving in mind his misfortunes, investigating the causes producing them, and deciding upon the forms of speech with which they would address him.

"Silence is a God," said the ancients, and terrible was it for Job to remain so long in his presence. The distressed features of his friends, their gestures, and

* Job ii. 11–13.

their glances, were interpreted by Job as having a significance greater by far than was meant; but they meant full enough.

Unable to endure their silence longer, he broke it, and gave expression to the agony torturing him, in terms startling and passionate.* He execrated the day of his birth, and, in almost tragic interrogation, asked why Providence had not done otherwise.†

* The following synopsis of the book of Job may be of service, especially in referring to the different addresses employed:—

					Chapters
Introductory narrative,					1, 2
Job's lament,					3
First controversy between Eliphaz and Job,					4—7
"	"	"	Bildad	"	8—10
"	"	"	Zophar	"	11—14
Second	"	"	Eliphaz	"	15—17
"	"	"	Bildad	"	18—19
"	"	"	Zophar	"	20—21
Third	"	"	Eliphaz	"	22—24
"	"	"	Bildad	"	25—26
"	"	"	Zophar	"	27—30
Elihu's address to Job,					31—37
Jehovah's	"				38—41
Conclusion,					42

† "Perish the day in which I was born,
And the night when they said, A man-child is brought forth.
O let that day be darkness!
May God from above never regard it;
Yea, let no sunshine come upon it.
Let darkness and the shadow of death cover it;
Let a spreading cloud hover over it;
Let it be frightened at its own deformity.

Of the three friends, Eliphaz the Temanite is the eldest, and the first to speak. His introductory address is marked with comparative self-restraint and mildness. He is, in this speech, a good representative of the true patriarchal chieftain, respectful, considerate,

"That night — let thick darkness seize it;
Let it not be joined to the days of the year,
Nor enter into the number of the months.
That night — may it be as a solitary rock;
Let no voice of joy ever come upon it!
Let the sorcerers of the day curse it,
Who are expert in conjuring up Leviathan.
Let the stars of its twilight be extinguished;
Let it long for light, but never reach it;
Let it never see the eyelids of the dawn:
Because it closed not the doors of the womb to me,
Nor shut out sorrow from mine eyes;
Or like an untimely birth I had perished,
Like abortions which never saw the light.
"O why did I not expire in the womb;
Why not perish in passing from the bowels?
Why was I received on the knees;
Why have I sucked the breasts?
I might now have lain still, and been quiet;
I might have gone to sleep, and been at rest,
Among the monarchs and despots of the earth,
Who built solitary mansions for themselves;
Or among chiefs, who abounded in gold,
Who glutted their storehouse with silver.
There the wicked cease to be a terror,
There the wearied are at rest.
The enslaved rest securely together,
They hear no more the taskmaster's voice.
There the small and the great are the same;
The slave is on a level with his dreaded lord.
"Why is light given to the wretched,

and dignified, yet with a slight tinge of censure, on account of the supposed sins of his friend.

But, as the controversy continued, he became extremely sophistical, and painfully severe, especially in

And life to the bitter in soul?
Who long for death, but find it not;
Who dig for it more than for hidden treasures;
Who rejoice even to exultation,
And triumph when they find the grave.
For God hath shut out death from a man,
To whom it would have been a repose.
For my groans anticipate my food,
My lamentations burst forth like a torrent.
For the terror which I dreaded has come upon me;
That which I feared has befallen me.
I have no tranquillity — I have no peace —
I have no rest — I am grievously distressed."
(Chap. iii. Wemyss' translation.)

Compare Jeremiah (xx. 14–18), Blayney's version: —

"Cursed be the day on which I was born:
The day on which my mother bare me, let it not be blessed.
Cursed be the man who brought the news to my father,
Saying, There is a male child born to thee,
Making him exceedingly glad.
And let the man be as the cities
Which Jehovah overthrew, and repented not;
Even hearing an outcry in the morning,
And an alarm at the time of noon.
Who did not slay me from the womb,
So that my mother might have been my grave,
Even the womb of her that conceived me, forever.
Wherefore came I forth from the womb,
To experience disquietude and sorrow,
And that my days should be spent in shame?"

his reference to the melancholy circumstances attending the loss of Job's children. And, towards the last, this pious friend insisted with almost furious harshness that these afflictions cannot be other than a just punishment for some secret sin of which Job had been guilty.

Eliphaz, like others aforetime, and some in aftertime, is mild, except in religious matters; but the crossing of his theological track was the signal for the appearance of a fiery zeal, which is often most violent in its persecutions. Some men would do quite well but for their religion.

Bildad the Shuhite is the second friend mentioned. From the start he attacked Job with keenness sharper than that of Eliphaz. He is eloquent and tragic; in a few passages, his descriptions are wrought up to the highest pitch of terror. He is less original than Eliphaz, and far less delicate. His expressions are often needlessly provoking and tantalizing. At times his charges upon Job are furious and awful.

Zophar, the third friend, presents strange diversities of character. He appears, at times, to be well nigh destitute of good sense, and mindless as to the propriety of things. He appears to delight in pointing out the effect of disease upon Job's countenance, which was needless and invidious.

On the other hand, his discourses upon the divine attributes are masterpieces of the grand and sublime. The vividness, too, with which the regulating and controlling hand of Providence in the affairs of men is depicted has rarely been equalled. He touched, however, upon nothing which had not been presented by the others. Taking his direction from Eliphaz chiefly, he was prepared, by what preceded, to pester his friend without mercy. He is the representative of a prejudiced, and, in some respects, narrow-minded bigot. He is an inveterate accuser. He repeated and exaggerated to the extreme what the others had said. At certain points, he seems cold, cruel, and heartless. It is not intended, doubtless, but is based upon misapprehension and mistaken zeal. The zeal of Zophar for the truth of God was indeed very great, for which, however, he got no thanks. God wants something besides zeal in his service.*

It was the very well-meant but wretched consolation of these men which put Job to the severest test. No other affliction seems to have equalled this. The friends meant well enough, like others, but, like others, were deluded. Their bad theology got the better of both their heads and hearts, and led them into mistakes which were well nigh the ruin of the man whom they had come to console. Not until the arrival of these friends was Job's self-composure, which had hitherto successfully withstood every kind of assault made upon it, in the least disturbed. There were heard no complaints of injustice; there were no questionings respecting the ways of Providence before this; but sick in body and sick in mind, and then presented by his friends with a cast-iron creed, and condemned because he would not accept and self-apply it, he was betrayed into saying some things which, it is true, had much better been left unsaid.

The creed of these Arabian princes was in their time general and popular. The Jewish people after-

* Psalms lxix. 9. John ii. 17.

wards adopted it. Job himself had held and taught it. And it is a little singular, even in our day, notwithstanding the light with which Christianity has flooded this world, that not a few rise up as its advocates. Certain positions in this creed are the following: There is an exact and uniform correspondence between sin and its punishment. Afflictions come because men have sinned. Misery always implies guilt. There is righteous retribution in this life, ounce for ounce; so much goodness, then so much happiness; so much sin, so much suffering.

Each of the friends, in turn, reiterated these points. Eliphaz introduced them, and made an implied application to Job.

"Remember, I pray thee, who ever perished, being innocent? or where were the righteous cut off? Even as I have seen, they that plough iniquity, and sow wickedness, reap the same. By the blast of God they perish, and by the breath of his nostrils are they consumed." (Chap. iv. 7–9.)

"I have seen the foolish taking root: but suddenly I cursed his habitation. His children are far from safety, and they are crushed in the gate, neither is there any to deliver them; whose harvest the hungry eateth up, and taketh it even out of the thorns, and the robber swalloweth up their substance. Affliction cometh not forth of the dust, neither doth trouble spring out of the ground." * (Chap. v. 3–6.)

* The following is Bildad's statement of the creed, and its application to Job, by implication at least: —

"Examine, I pray thee, former generations;
Inform thyself of the wisdom of their ancestors:

Job, in the mean time, had confessed his common human frailty; but that these dire misfortunes had come upon him in consequence of his sin, — he knew better. He repelled their insinuations with indigna-

(For we are but of yesterday, and have no experience;
Our days on the earth are but a shadow.)
Shall they not teach thee and instruct thee,
And from the heart utter maxims like these? —
"'Can the papyrus grow without water?
Can the bulrush grow without moisture?
While it is yet shooting, it languishes,
And withers before it has perfected its herbage:
Such are the paths of all that forget God;
So perisheth the hope of the profligate.'
"Lo! such is the catastrophe of the wicked,
And others shall arise in his place.
But God will not reject the upright,
Nor will he strengthen the hands of evil-doers.
Even yet he may fill thy mouth with laughter,
And thy lips with merriment.
Thine enemies shall be clothed with shame,
And the dwelling of the wicked shall come to nought."
(viii. 8–14, 19–22.)

Zophar expands and insinuates, but adds nothing new.

"Ha! knowest thou not this — from of old,
Since the time when man was placed upon the earth —
That the triumph of the wicked is soon over,
And the joy of the impious is but for a moment?
Though his pride should mount up to heaven,
And his head reach to the clouds;
Even amidst his splendor he shall perish forever:
Those who once knew him shall say, 'Where is he?'
He shall disappear as a dream that cannot be traced;
He shall vanish like a spectre in the night.
The eye that caught a glance at him shall see him no more;

tion. Their charges rolled past him as dismal mockery. Do you suppose, he seems to say, that I will acknowledge sins which I have not committed? Away with you and your creed!

His place shall no more behold him.
His children shall be reduced to beggary,
And constrained to restore that which he had seized.
His bones shall be filled with secret lusts;
He shall lie down in the dust with his sins.
"Though wickedness was sweet to his taste,
Though it was hid under his tongue,
Though he indulged it, and would not give it up,
But would retain it still in his palate,
His food shall be changed in his bowels,
To the gall of asps in his stomach.
He shall vomit the wealth which he devoured;
God shall expel it from his bowels.
He shall suck the poison of asps;
The tongue of the viper shall destroy him.
He shall no more behold the brooks,
The streams flowing with milk and honey.
What he seized he shall restore without reservation,
Nor shall he enjoy the wealth he had acquired.
"Because he oppressed the orphans of the poor,
And pulled down houses which he had not built;
Because his appetite could not be satisfied,
Nor did he refuse anything to his lusts;
He set no bounds to his voracity;
Therefore his happiness shall not be permanent.
Amidst the fulness of his tyranny he shall be in straits;
All manner of distress shall come upon him.
Even when his appetite is satiated,
God shall send on him the fury of his wrath,
And rain it upon him while he is eating.
Should he flee from the iron weapon,
The bow of brass shall strike him through;

Job acknowledged that, sooner or later, the wicked are brought to justice, but insisted, nevertheless, without qualification, that in the short run, at least, there is not, in this life, anything like a just distribution of rewards and punishments.*

The arrow shall pierce through his body,
The glittering shaft through his gall.
He shall die, oppressed with terrors;
Calamities of all kinds are treasured up for him.
A fire unblown shall consume him;
What remained in his tent shall be destroyed.
The heaven shall reveal his iniquity,
The earth shall rise up against him.
The increase of his house shall roll away,
Like torrents, in the day of indignation.
Such is the portion of the wicked from God,
And such his heritage from the Deity." (xx. 4-30.)

* "It is a singular thing, that I should come to this conclusion,
'That God punishes alike the innocent and guilty.'
Though he slays fools with his scourge,
He also smiles at the calamities of the just.
He abandons a land to the violence of the wicked;
The face of their judges is hoodwinked,
That they turn not to say, Who has done this?"
(ix. 22-24.)

"The tents of plunderers are secure;
Secure are the abodes of them who provoke God,
Whose power is to them instead of a God.
But now, inquire of the beasts, and they will teach you,
And the fowls of the air, and they will explain to you,
And the shrubs of the earth, and they will show you,
And the fishes of the sea will declare it to you:
Who amongst all these does not know,
That all things are arranged by the power of God?

Failing to convince Job of the unqualified truth of their creed, and not succeeding, through these gentler methods, in drawing out from the patriarch confessions of personal guilt, these friends proceeded to make their own application, and charged no longer by insinuation, but directly and furiously, upon Job all the iniquity which his aggravated afflictions, according to their views, demanded.

They began by strongly hinting that it was probable that enormous secret guilt lay at the bottom of these sufferings; they then advanced farther and farther, inquisitor-like, until at length they told him that they believed his life had been hypocritical and iniquitous.

In whose hand is the soul of every living creature,
And the breath of all mankind." (xii. 6–10.)
"Why do the impious live happy,
Grow old, and abound in wealth?
Their offspring are established before them,
And their posterity before their eyes.
Their houses are safe from fear;
They are not scourged with the Divine rod.
Their cattle are fruitful and active;
Their kine bring forth, and do not cast their young.
They send forth their little ones like a flock,
And their children leap for joy.
They rise up to the tabor and harp,
They trip merrily to the sound of the pipe.
They pass their life happily,
And descend quietly to the tomb.
Though they had said to God, 'Depart from us,
We desire not the knowledge of thy ways!
Who is the Almighty, that we should worship him?
And what avails it to address him in prayer?'
Lo, such do not enjoy constant happiness." (xxi. 7–16.)

They accused him with meriting to the full extent, and more than meriting, the misfortunes he bore. They looked upon him as a blasphemer, gazing upon him, at times, with something akin to awe and terror.

How could they do less? To give up their splendid system of theology, they could not. Calamities are the fruit of sin, they reiterated. "You are suffering calamities; therefore you are a sinner. Terrible calamities are the fruit of terrible sin; you are suffering terrible calamities, therefore you are a terrible sinner." *

* As specimens of these accusations are the following: —

"Then Eliphaz the Temanite again took up the discourse:
'Does it become a wise man to give unsolid answers,
And to swell his breast with the east wind?
To refute arguments by proving nothing,
And to use unprofitable words?
Thou thyself castest off piety,
And weakenest prayers directed to God.
Thine own words show thine iniquity,
Though thou usest the tongue of the crafty.
Thine own mouth condemns thee, not I;
Thine own lips testify against thee.
Wert thou the first man that was born?
Wert thou formed before the mountains?
Hast thou listened in the privy council of God,
And drawn away wisdom to thyself?
What knowest thou, that we know not?
Or understandest thou, of which we are ignorant?
The hoary-headed and the ancient are among us,
More venerable for years than thy father.
Dost thou undervalue the Divine consolations,
Or the addresses of kindness to thyself?
To what pitch of boldness would thy heart carry thee —

They really knew no actual evil in Job, but they thought there must be. To make good their opinion, and support their pet theories, they converted conjecture into certainty. "Of course he has committed

At what have thine eyes taken aim —
That thou shouldst let loose thy mind against God,
And cast forth such words from thy mouth?
Where is the man who is pure,
The offspring of woman who is blameless?
Behold, in his holy ones he cannot place confidence,
The heavens are not clean in his sight.
How abominable and impure then must man be,
Who drinketh iniquity like water!
"'Listen to me, and I will tell thee —
What I have seen, I will relate;
Which sages have proclaimed,
As a matter known in the time of their ancestors,
To whom alone the land was given,
When no stranger had come amongst them: —
"'All the days of the wicked he is his own tormentor,
And a reckoning of years is laid up for the violent.
A sound of alarm rings in his ears;
Even in peace the despoiler invades him.
He cannot hope to escape from darkness;
Even from the lurking-place the sword awaits him.
He wanders about, and becomes the prey of vultures;
He knows the evil day is prepared for him.
Distress and danger dismay him;
They oppress him like a tyrant.
He is destined to the heaviest sufferings,
Because he stretched forth his hand against God,
And acted haughtily towards the Almighty.
God shall press upon him with extended neck,
Through the mailed bosses of his own buckler.
Though his face be enveloped with fat,
Though he heaped up fat on his loins,

sin," they said. "Of course, of course." These opinions they felt they must cling to, though the heavens fall. To defend them they exhausted their stores of rhetoric; they alternated between irony, sarcasm,

Yet in desolate cities he shall dwell;
Houses to be deserted by him,
Which are destined to be reduced to ashes.
He shall not grow rich, nor have permanent wealth,
Nor shall he be master of his own desires.
He shall not escape from darkness;
The lightning shall wither his green shoots;
He shall be carried away by a wind sent from above.
Let him not trust to his own prosperity;
An unhappy change shall take place in his affairs:
Before his season it shall be accomplished,
Nor shall his branch flourish.
He shall cast his unripe fruit like the vine,
And shall shed his blossoms like the olive.
The house of the wicked shall be a barren rock;
Fire shall consume the tents of the ungodly.
Pregnant with mischief, they bring forth crime,
And carry deceit in their womb.'" (xv. 1–35.)

"Is not thy wickedness sufficiently great?
Yea, there is no bound to thine iniquities.
Thou hast unjustly taken a pledge from thy brethren,
Thou hast stripped the destitute of their garments.
Thou hast not refreshed with water the weary,
Thou hast refused bread to the hungry.
Thou hast suffered the man of power to seize the land,
And the man of authority to take possession of it.
Thou hast sent widows empty away,
And hast bruised the orphans' arms.
Therefore thou art surrounded with snares,
And sudden ruin alarms thee.
Thy light is changed into darkness,
And a flood of waters covers thee.

and crimination; they appealed to experience and antiquity; they explored all the wealth of Arabian wisdom, employing trite maxims and sage sentences,

Truly, God is higher than the heavens,
And sees the topmost stars, however lofty:
How then dost thou say, 'Can God know?
Can he discern those things which are transacted in darkness?
Thick clouds enclose him, that he cannot see;
He walks on the convexity of the heavens.'
"Hast thou observed the ancient tract,
Which was trodden by wicked mortals;
Who perished by a sudden death,
Whose foundation is a molten flood?
Who said to God, 'Depart from us, —
What can the Almighty do to us?'
Though he had filled their houses with wealth.
(Far from me be their wicked conduct!)
The righteous beheld and rejoiced;
The innocent derided them, saying,
'Surely their substance was carried away,
And a fire consumed their riches.'
"Turn therefore to Him, and be an upright man;
So shalt thou have abundant produce.
Receive the law from his mouth,
And store up his sayings in thy mind.
If thou return to the Almighty, thou shalt be restored,
If thou put away all iniquity from thy tent."

(xxii. 5–23.)

"Then Bildad of Shuah interposed and said:
'How long wilt thou utter such things,
And thy sayings burst forth like an impetuous wind?
Will God pervert justice?
Will the Almighty pass an unrighteous judgment?
If thy children have sinned against him,
He hath cast them off on account of their transgressions.

adorning them with the aptest and most beautiful metaphor and poetry.

Job, on the other hand, continued to repel their

If thou wouldst seek betimes unto God,
And make thy supplication to the Almighty,
Provided thou wert just and upright,
Even yet he would rise up for thee,
And prosper the abode of thine integrity;
And though thy beginning were small,
Thy latter end would be very prosperous." (viii. 1-7.)
"How long will ye discourse captiously?
Be temperate; and then let us speak.
Why dost thou regard us as brutes?
Why should we appear contemptible before thee?
Thou tearest thyself in thy fury:
Shall the earth be deserted for thee?
Shall the rocks be removed from their place?
The light of the wicked shall be extinguished;
The flame of his fire shall not shine.
Daylight shall be darkness in his tent;
His lamp shall be extinguished over him.
The steps of his strength shall be straitened,
His own counsel shall subvert him.
He is caught by the feet in a pitfall;
Perfidious snares encompass him.
The trap shall lay hold of his heel,
It shall fasten thoroughly upon him.
A cord is hid for him in the ground,
And a gin under his path.
Terrors await him on all sides,
They force him to retrace his steps.
His strength shall be enfeebled by hunger,
Destruction shall march at his side.
The first-born of death shall devour his skin,
It shall greedily feed on his members,

charges; he answered back by appealing to history and experience; he argued his case vehemently; he chastised his opponents with keen irony (xii. 2); then

Confidence shall be expelled from his dwelling,
Terror shall seize him as a king.
It will make its abode in his tent,
Nor shall anything be left there.
Sulphur shall be rained upon his dwelling.
Below, his roots shall be dried up;
Above, his branches shall be withered.
His memory shall be effaced from the land,
And no trace of him found among foreigners.
They shall drive him from daylight into darkness,
And hunt him out of the world.
He shall have neither son nor kinsman amongst his people,
Nor any one remaining amongst his possessions.
The west shall be astonished at his end,
The east shall be panic-struck.
Such are the dwellings of the impious man;
Such the state of him who despises God." (xviii. 1–21.)

"Then Zophar the Naamathite answered in these terms:

'He who speaketh much should be replied to,
Otherwise the talkative man would appear to be right.
If others heard thy boasting in silence,
Thou mightest mock on without contradiction.
Thou sayest, "My conscience is clear,
And I am pure in thine eyes," (addressing God.)
I wish God would indeed speak to thee,
And open his lips against thee;
That he would unfold to thee the secrets of wisdom:
Then wouldst thou have double reason to remain tranquil;
Then thou wouldst know that God hath forborne
A portion of the chastisement thou deservest.'"

(xi. 1–6.)

implored their pity, and then declared his freedom from all intentional sin, in language both singularly beautiful and impressive.*

* "'Doth not the Eternal see my ways,
And number all my footsteps?
"'If I have acted fraudulently,
And my foot hath hastened to dishonesty,
Let me be weighed in a just balance,
That God may know mine integrity.
If my step hath turned out of the way,
And my heart gone astray after mine eyes,
If any bribe hath cleaved to my hands,
Then let me sow, and let another eat;
Let another root out what I have planted.
"'If my heart hath been enticed to a married woman,
Or I have lain in wait at my neighbor's door,
Then let my wife gratify another,
And let others bow down upon her.
For this is the basest wickedness,
And a crime to be punished by the Judge.
It is a fire consuming to destruction;
It would root out all mine increase.
"'If I denied justice to my man-servant,
Or to my maid-servant, when they disputed with me —
What then shall I do, when God maketh inquest?
When he inquires, what answer should I make?
Did not He who formed me form them?
Were we not fashioned alike in the womb?
"'If I withheld from the poor what they asked,
Or have grieved the eyes of the widow,
Or have eaten my morsel alone,
And the orphan hath not partaken with me —
(Whereas from my youth I nourished them as a father,
And was the widow's guide from my earliest years) —
If I have seen any perish for want of clothing,
Or any poor man without raiment;

Thus this controversial football flew backward and forward. "These ten times," exclaimed the patriarch, "these ten times have ye reproached me." No wonder

If his loins have not blessed me,
Nor himself been warmed with the wool of my sheep;
If I have raised a hand against the orphan,
Because I saw I had authority in the gate —
May my shoulder-bone be dislocated,
And my arm be broken at the elbow!
No! — the fear of God's judgments overawed me;
I could do nothing before his majesty.
"'If I have made gold my reliance,
And have said to fine gold, "Thou art my trust;"
If I exulted when my wealth was great,
When my hand found vast riches;
"'If my own land exclaim against me;
If its furrows make complaint;
If I have consumed its produce without wages,
Or have deprived my hirelings of their reward, —
Let my land produce thistles instead of wheat,
And poisonous weeds instead of barley.
"'If I have looked at the sun when he shone,
Or the moon, advancing in brightness;
And my heart has been secretly enticed,
And my hand has borne a kiss to my mouth —
This would have been a crime deserving to be judged,
For I should have denied the Supreme God.
"'If I have triumphed in the destruction of my enemy,
Or leaped with joy when harm befell him,
(Whereas I suffered not my mouth to sin,
By imprecating evil upon him) —
"'If my domestics were not wont to say,
"Who is there that hath not been filled with his dainties?"
The stranger lodged not in the street;
My door was open to every comer.
"'If, human-like, I concealed my sin,

that during this encounter, he was occasionally exasperated. Singular is it that these friends, who had come to offer consolation, were comforters ("miserable comforters are ye all"), worse, ten times over, than the black leprosy; worse, in fact, than the devil had been, and a much greater trial.

A greater trial than the devil had been, did we say? Nay, Satan was personally in this last affliction, likewise. No more visible is his trail in the losses and sickness of Job, than in this visit of these pious but deluded friends. The narrative, it is true, leaves us to infer his presence. But he is the inveterate accuser of every afflicted one.* There is no calamity on earth where he, or some of his minions, are not present. God permits, but the devil deals the blow and God heals the wound, and brings good out of it, are the lessons of Job's life, and of every life.

And hid my transgression in my bosom,
Let me be confounded before the multitude;
Let me be covered with public contempt;
Let me be dumb, nor dare to go abroad.
"'O that God would deign to hear me!
This is my declaration — let the Almighty reply to it!
Let my opponent write down the charge:
Surely I would wear it on my shoulder;
I would bind it round me like a diadem;
I would disclose to him the number of my steps;
I would approach him with the boldness of a prince.'
Thus far are the discourses of Job." (xxx. 4–40.)

* The word by which Satan is here designated signifies the *Troubler;* and Job, *Hiob*, signifies the *Much Persecuted.* We may note also that Satan is adroit, often putting an angel of light in his place to do his work. In general, he does his meanest work by proxy. (Gen. iii. 1–6.)

In some countries the judge delivers his severest sentence with a curtain drawn between his face and that of the condemned. In the most terrific struggle which God's children encounter, no hand or foot is visible; friends may be near; surroundings may be sunlit, but the encounter is within the soul; it is a silent but awful war which there rages. Many were the afflictions of the patriarch, and skilful was the master of such tactics, who brought these fierce battalions against him.

When Job was wounded as a deer in the chase, when he was worn down and almost worn out with pain, — sick as he could be and live, — it was that malignant *troubler* whose hand smote him.

When harassed with his own doubts, his brain in a perpetual craze, and his soul whelmed in that mystery which multiplies dangers and magnifies distress by as much as the cause is unknown, — as the hand which wrote before Belshazzar was terrible because it was naked and had no body, — yes, in that hour it was this same *satanic troubler* who plunged the patriarch into the horrors of nightmare and delirium, this blackness of darkness.

And when these Arabian friends touched him in the most sensitive spot; when they attacked his integrity and good name, upon which, life-long, he had prided himself; when they piled their solemn and pious falsehoods up against him, mountain high; when he was assaulted as a sinner of blackest heart, pronounced an extortioner and a scourger of poor people, a pretended saint, but a skilled hypocrite, and an enemy of Jehovah, — in this hardest encounter of all, when God seemed to say, "This is your hour, and the power of darkness," then, too, it was this same *infernal troubler* who was permitted to give points and barbs, destitute of all feeling and pity, to those fiery darts which entered the soul of the "*much troubled*," and to those rebukes which were none the less distracting because uttered with pious and religious intention.

Satan did his worst. Death would have been relief. Infidelity began to raise its towering structure. No wonder that Job's human nature came to the surface; he would not have been man had he remained self-poised. The language spoken was fitful, bold, and defiant; how could it have been otherwise? What fitter expression could there be for uncontrollable anguish, bitterness of spirit and fiendish torture? His complaints are the exactest symbol possible of the wild, vehement, desperate, and reckless outgush of terrific and satanic suffering.*

* Striking illustrations are the following passages: —

"Am I a sea or a great whale
That thou settest a guard over me?
O, release me, since my days are vanity!
What is man, that thou shouldst sustain him,
And shouldst pay attention to him;
That thou shouldst visit him every morning,
And prove him every moment?
Why wilt thou not turn away from me,
Nor let me alone till I draw my breath?
Have I sinned? What injury have I done to thee,
O thou Observer of men?
Why set me up as a mark to shoot at,
So that I am become a burden to myself?
Why not pardon my transgression?

The visit of these friends was the crisis in his trial. Everything, in those few days, was to be gained or

Why not take away mine iniquity,
That now I might lie down in the dust?
In the morning thou wouldst seek me; but I should be gone." (vii. 12, 17–21.)
"He who from his whirlwind hath bruised me,
And has multiplied my wounds without cause,
He hath not allowed me time to breathe,
But loadeth me constantly with new sorrows.
"It is a singular thing that I should come to this conclusion, —
'That God punishes alike the innocent and guilty.'
Though he slays fools with his scourge,
He also smiles at the calamities of the just.
He abandons a land to the violence of the wicked;
The face of their judges is hoodwinked,
That they turn not to say, Who has done this?
"Grant, then, that I am wicked!
Why should I therefore labor in vain?
Should I wash myself in snow-water,
And cleanse my hands in purity,
Still wouldst thou plunge me into filth,
So that my own clothes would abhor me.
He is not a man like myself whom I could reply to,
That we should come together before the judge.
There is no arbitrator between us,
To exert his authority over both.
Let him take away his rod from me,
And no longer alarm me by his terror;
Then I might speak, and not be afraid of him,
But at present I stand not upon equal terms."
(ix. 17, 18, 22–24, 29–35.)
"I am thoroughly weary of my life;
I will abandon myself to my complaints;
I will speak in the bitterness of my soul.

lost; for everything was staked upon that final trial.

I will say to God, 'Do not condemn me;
Show me wherefore thou contendest with me!
Can it give thee pleasure to oppress me;
To reject the work of thine own hands,
And to favor the counsel of the wicked!
Are thine eyes like those of mortals?
Seest thou as man seeth?
Are thy days as the days of a man,
Or thy years like human life;
That thou searchest out mine iniquity,
And makest inquest for my sin?
Though thou knowest that I am not impious.—
"'Elated like a lion, thou springest upon me,
And again thou showest thy power over me.
Thou renewest thy tormenting attacks upon me,
Thou increasest thy vexation against me,
Fresh harasses and conflicts are with me;
Pray spare me, that I may enjoy some repose,
Before I go, whence I shall not return,
To a land of gloom, and the shadow of death,
To a land of dissolution and extinction,
Of the shadow of death, where there is no order,
And where the very light is as pitchy darkness.'"

(x. 1–7, 16, 17, 21, 22.)

"Hold your peace, for I must speak —
I will, whatever it should cost me.
Come what may, I will take my flesh in my teeth,
And carry my life in my own hand.
There! let him kill me — I have nothing to hope for.
"Why dost thou hide thy face,
And treat me as an enemy?
Why break a poor, driven leaf?
Why pursue the dry stubble?
Thou writest severe decisions against me,
Thou imputest to me the sins of my youth.

"Thus far, and no farther," is the constantly repeated injunction of Jehovah. He interposes oftener than men imagine. Afterwards the angels come to minister. But it is hard that a man must fight his way alone, when many another man might lend a hand. Would to God that charity were not so rare among even the best of folks. Many a cup of bitterness has been unintentionally placed to the lips already enough sorrowful.

Let each take care how he consoles his friend. When the heart is already bruised it is easy to bruise it more. The water that cools and refreshes at one time, scalds and burns to death at another. And it

Thou puttest my feet in confinement,
Thou narrowly observest all my movements,
Thou brandest the soles of my feet.
Me, who am already consumed with putrefaction,
Like a garment corroded by the moth."
(xiii. 13–15, 24–28.)

"God hath delivered me over to the wicked;
He hath hurled me into the hands of the impious.
I was in tranquillity, but he disturbed me;
Seizing me by the neck he throws me on the ground.
He sets me up as a mark;
His archers surround me;
One transfixes my reins, and does not spare;
Another poureth out my gall upon the ground:
He breaketh me with breach upon breach,
He runneth upon me like a giant." (xvi. 11–14.)

"I cry to thee (my God), but thou hearest me not;
I stand up, but thou dost not regard me.
Thou art become an adversary to me;
Thou makest war on me with thy strong arm.
Thou liftest me up in the air,
Thou makest me ride on the storm;
Then thou dashest me to the ground. (xxix. 20–22.)

were always far better to have an eye that sees beyond the present inch. "There are more things in heaven and earth than are dreamt of in your philosophy." We cannot tell what one is, religiously or morally, by his present prosperities or adversities; we must hear what goes on in heaven before giving our decisions.

Much that is parable hangs about this world. To pronounce one sinful because in trouble, gives the lie to Gethsemane.

"Who did sin," asked the Jews of Christ, "this man or his parents, that he was born blind?" Of course, one or the other. "*Neither!*" replied our Saviour; "but that the works of God should be made manifest in him." Earthquakes, lightnings, tempests, pestilences, conflagrations,—do they destroy sinners only, and do they come merely because the victims themselves are guilty? Fearful is such a creed!

Suppose ye that those Galileans whose blood Pilate mingled with their sacrifices, or those eighteen upon whom the tower in Siloam fell and slew, or those who are wrecked at sea, or those who are crushed and scalded in railway disasters, are sinners more than all others in Jerusalem and elsewhere? "I tell ye, Nay." *

The thoroughly vicious and corrupt man is, no doubt, miserable enough. But men equally selfish, whose fine senses are duly gratified, are fairly well off in this world, say what we may against it. A degree of happiness is compatible, in this life, with considerable iniquity. The really malignant vapors do not infect the air until after sun-fall.

* Luke xiii. 1-5.

The good man's goodness, on the other hand, is not a continuous sunshine. Inward consolations are rich, but not everything. Wounds smart on a good man, and need healing. The poppy, each spring-time, may well be planted in every man's garden. Job was not happy on the ash-heap, the butt of ridicule and the mock of scorn, like some old stump of a tree, "which the lightning has scathed, rotting away in the wind and rain."

The fact is, God admits men to his service, not upon conditions of either rewarding them at present with happiness, or shielding them from adversity. He sends his rain upon the just and the unjust. He reserves the right to give or withhold. We ask, Why? — why this or that, — but find no answer. Faithfulness to God and truth "are higher and better than happiness, though they are attended with wounded feet and bleeding brows, and hearts loaded down with sorrow." Men must learn to serve without looking too sharply to the pay for it. Their business is to do what is right, and ask no questions as to what comes of it; be it one thing or another, it is no very mighty matter. The veil which, in the legend, lay before the face of Isis, is not to be raised — till the day after doomsday. God wants men to love him, whether made more comfortable or not by it.

Is that love, it is often asked, which influences man or woman to ask the hand of another, *because* a more comfortable home will be gained thereby. No wonder courts are crowded with divorce petitions.

If need be, like the Norsemen, God's servants every day must fashion their "sword-hilts into crosses," and become themselves an unpaid, crusading chivalry, to go anywhere and do anything.

Is it asked, too, about trials, — the trials in our own hearts and homes? We cannot always tell. One gains not much by questioning the unquestionable, especially when the eyes are blind and the ears deaf.

God is an artist; the greatest artists work by night; they shut themselves by day in a darkened room, and chisel the marble by the light of a solitary and dim candle. There is, now and then, a ray of light in the deepest earthly gloom; enough to show that trials sometimes serve one a good turn: besides leaving in their path much rich fruit, they leave the one disciplined much more of a man.*

The high-borns, as we are often reminded, unless

* Dr. South, after showing that it was not for Job's sin that God afflicted him, but because he was freely pleased to do so, says, "Yet there was a reason of this pleasure, which was to discover that grace of patience, given him by God, to the astonishment of the world and the confutation of the devil; whom we find so impudent as to beat God down to his face, that he had never a servant in the world who would suffer such things from him without sinning against him. And was it not worth the sitting upon a dunghill, and seeing his substance scattered, his children struck dead, and himself mocked in his misery, to vindicate the honor of that God, who gave him all of these things, from the devil, the true common enemy? and to be recorded as a mirror of patience to all posterity? and to convince the world that there is something in virtue better than possessions, truer than friends, and stronger than Satan? Though this dealing was not an effect of God's vindictive justice, but of his absolute power, yet it equally served both God's glory and Job's advantage."

they learn where poor men live, and know the chores poor men do, unless they feel danger, cold, hunger, war, or something else, will have moderate ideas.* Barley crusts are better than too much cake and sweetmeats. The better part of our best education we have no schoolmasters for; and that which most promotes our advancement is never noted in our text books.†

Good health is considered a boon, but it is not always religious; sickness sometimes sanctifies, health sometimes carnalizes.

"Chamber of sickness! 'Midst thy silence, oft
A voice is heard,
Which, though it fall like dew on flowers, so soft,
Yet speaks each word
Into the aching heart's unseen recess,
With power no earthly accents could possess."

"The happy periods of human history," says Hegel, "are its least fruitful ones." The way to become immortal is to die daily.

* Emerson.

† De Quincey expresses a similar idea very beautifully: —

"Now the word *educo*, with the penultimate short, was derived (by a process often exemplified in the crystallization of language) from the word *educo*, with the penultimate long. Whatsoever *educes*, or develops, *educates*. By the education, therefore, is meant, not the poor machinery that moves by spelling-books and grammars, but by that mighty system of central forces hidden in the deep bosom of human life, which by passion, by strife, by temptation, by the energies of resistance, works forever upon children, resting not day or night, any more than the mighty wheel of day and night themselves, whose moments, like restless spokes, are glimmering forever as they revolve."

But far more than this: trials bring man face to face with God. They set his house apart from the world for a season, and lift him outside the earth, with nothing between his soul and the eternal. The crape on the door-knob, could it speak, would say, "No admittance. Go on, stranger; God is here for an hour or more." Wonderful is this acquired or inspired power of dealing with appearances.

It is the shock which throws the liquid in the retort into beautiful crystals. It is the earthquake that shakes down the miser's old house, and out from the crannies roll the stockings full of shining coin.* No man knows how much of a man he is until he has been fairly struck.

"We learn geology," says Emerson, "the morning after earthquakes; on ghastly diagrams of cloven mountains, upheaved plains, and dry beds of the sea." Such are God's opportunities and ways of disclosing himself; and marvellous are the revelations he sometimes makes. The thing to guard against is, that losses, crosses, and surprises, born of spiritual thunderstorms and earthquakes, leave not the soul withered or withering as under a curse.

It is the tornado that clears the atmosphere, though in its march it levels the house as well as freights off deadly contagions. Be patient; bear the grief that is crushing life out, just as well as you can. More is pending than you dream of. Perhaps God would have you, too, prove that Satan is a liar. There is a world somewhere, doubtless, that wants a king. This which we see is often the type, prelude, and pledge

* Holmes.

of eternal restoration. At least we can depend upon being helped to repair the house, and out from the tempest — this sackcloth tempest — a sun will rise anon, and there shall be no more night. "A joyful issue is that when no one concerned receives ultimate harm save Satan himself."

Most storms clear up in night-time, or towards evening. As with every brood of trials, so with these in the case of Job, there is an end at length, and it comes often in ways unexpected, and when matters are at their worst. A few things, meantime, cannot fail to have been noticed. Job succeeded, at last, in silencing his opponents. They said less and less, he more and more; and in the closing interview he proceeded uninterrupted, "with calm confidence, like a lion among his defeated enemies."

There is found, also, over against everything questionable in his expression, a full offset of something commendable. He asked, complainingly, Why is the divine will thus, and not otherwise? then submitted, saying, Not my will, but thine, be done. He demanded justice as one crushed without cause, then implored pity merely as a suppliant. He complained that God deals with unmerciful severity, then poured out his confession as a child to a tender father. One moment the surges dashed almost over his head, and pitiful is his wail of despair; the next moment the waves were curling their crests beneath his feet, and he reaffirmed his confidence that God will make it all right in the end. At times he was irritated and violent; a moment later, calm as an inland lake when the winds are whist. He loved his life, but in his distress he longed for death. He smiled as the door of the sepulchre opened, but started back with a shudder as its cold, damp atmosphere touched him. How masterly human!

A change in Job for the better is also noticeable throughout. As the controversy with his friends continued, he seemed the more and more easily to tread his temptations under his feet. He found in them a ladder on which his spirit climbed above the clouds. He saw things clearer and clearer. The thick scales fell from his eyes. He passed farther and farther from his friends, soaring, at length, where their imaginations even could not follow. Their condition, on the other hand, grew darker and darker; they exhausted their stock of argument, and were gradually reduced to silence; calmness of tone followed; and the storm of passion was stilled now that those who stirred it no longer spoke.

There is of a sudden a presentiment that we are upon the threshold of solution. Bildad spoke, and should have been followed by Zophar; but for some reason there was general silence.

A new personage appeared; he had been burning to speak, but the etiquette of the East forbade him. He was a young man, and wise beyond his years;* he

* "Why he is described as a youth may be learned from the words which the author puts into his mouth: —

"'I thought, Let days speak, and let the multitude of years prove wisdom.' But the Spirit is in man [on that all depends!], and the breath of the Almighty giveth them under-

was able to throw much new light upon the dark problems among which the others had blindly groped. He declared what was no doubt true, that Job had not been faultless under his trials; no man is, or has been, such, or beyond the possibility, under severe temptation, of becoming almost one knows not what.

No man, did we say? No man save one, — he of Nazareth, we mean.* A faultless life from first to last concerns God less, perhaps, than a constant strug-

standing. Not the many are wise: neither do the aged understand judgment. Majorities are without weight in the church, and in spiritual things age does not at all carry the weight which belongs to it in the walks of common life. *One* inexperienced youth, *with* the spirit of God, is wiser than loud multitudes and gray heads, and even than the Coryphæi of wisdom without it. Besides, a youth is the most fitting representative of a truth which is here introduced with freshness and vigor into the midst of the church of God." — HENGSTENBERG.

* Elihu's description of the tempest is a piece of almost unequalled magnificence: —

"With his hands he grasps the lightning,
And gives his orders where it shall fall.
He commands that his friends should be safe,
But he hurls his wrath against the wicked.
Truly, at this my heart trembles,
And shudders in my bosom.
Hear with awe the concussion of his voice,
And the peal that issues from his mouth.
Throughout the whole heaven is its flash,
And its blaze to the ends of the earth.
After it pealeth the roar,
He thundereth with his majestic voice.
The peals succeed without intermission,
Yet no one can trace him, though his voice be heard."

gle through life for faultlessness. The parables of the wandering sheep and the lost piece of money are suggestive.

But this should be noted, that throughout that night of gloom, even when reason had well nigh quit its throne, we listen in vain to hear anything from the patriarch that has the curse of God in it.

Job had, it is true, complained — complained most bitterly; but chiefly because of an impenetrable gloom. He was no rebellious spirit, struck down in his haughty pride: he was no defiant infidel, who calls God "the Almighty tyrant, whom he wishes to look boldly in the face, and swear that his evil is not good;" he was no stoic, who *could* bear because he *must* bear the blow struck; he was no Titan, contending in rage with the gods; he was no Prometheus, bound to a rock because Jove had been displeased and was the stronger; but Job was a man, — a tender and noble man; weak, to be sure, but continually struggling to overcome every weakness; self-confident, it is true, but awaiting any correction, if from the hand of God. He was ignorant of many things, it is true, but still a worthy man, left for a season to suffer for God's glory and the good of others, but during every moment of his trial dearly beloved of God, as justly he should have been.

The needle had only been shaken by a violent hand from its bearings. It quickly returned, and regained its native north. Among the sublimest sentiments ever uttered are these that sprang from this afflicted hero's many sorrows, even when most sorrowful. Like beautiful flowers on the turf of the grave-mound, they will bloom, and bloom on, forever and ever. Listen: "Though he slay me, yet will I trust him." *

"As God liveth, who hath taken away my judgment; and the Almighty, who hath vexed my soul; all the while my breath is in me, and the spirit of God is in my nostrils; my lips shall not speak wickedness, nor my tongue utter deceit; till I die I will not remove mine integrity from me. My righteousness I hold fast, and will not let it go; my heart shall not reproach me so long as I live.†

"For I know that my Redeemer liveth, and that he shall stand at the latter day upon the earth: and though after my skin worms destroy this body, yet in my flesh shall I see God: whom I shall see for myself, and mine eyes shall behold, and not another; though my reins be consumed within me." ‡ Here

* Job xiii. 15. † Job xvii. 2-6.

‡ Job xix. 25-27. His magnificent eulogy of Wisdom should not be overlooked.

"Wisdom! whence then cometh it?
  Where is the abode of understanding?
It is hid from the eyes of the living;
It is concealed from the fowls of the air.
Destruction and death say,
'We have heard of its fame with our ears.'
God alone understandeth its track;
Yea, he is acquainted with its abode.
For he seeth to the extremities of the earth;
He surveyeth under the whole heavens.
When he made a balance for the air,
And adjusted the waters by measure —
When he fixed a course for the rain,
And a path for the lightning of the storm —

is the embodiment of nobility. This is the blood of no common man; and yet the blood of a common man is convertible, by process of trial and the grace of God, into blood the most royal. He, whoever he is, that is faithful over a few things shall be made ruler over many.

A thunder-storm rose in the distance; it drew nearer and nearer; a profound silence rested upon all nature; an awful peal was heard, the cloud burst, and the majestic voice of the Almighty was heard, uttering words that well befit so sublime a speaker,*

> Then he saw it and proclaimed it;
> He established it and thoroughly proved it.
> And to man he said — 'Behold!
> The fear of Jehovah, that is wisdom!
> And to abstain from evil — is understanding!'"
> (xxviii. 20-28.)

* The following observations will doubtless receive full indorcement of the reader: —

"I imagine," says Scott, "it will be easily granted, that, for majesty of sentiment and strength of expression, this speech has nothing equal to it in the most admired productions of Greece and Rome." "To put suitable language in the mouth of the Deity," says Gilfillan, "has generally tasked to straining, or crushed to feebleness the genius of poets. Homer, indeed, at times nobly ventriloquizes from the top of Olympus; but it *is* ventriloquism! Homer's thunder, not Jove's. Milton, while impersonating God, falls flat; he peeps and mutters from the dust; he shrinks from seeking to fill up the compass of the Eternal's voice. Adequately to represent God speaking required not only the highest inspiration, but that the poet had heard, or thought that he heard, His very voice, sharpening articulate sounds from the midnight torrent, from the voices of the wind, from the chambers of thunder, from the rush of the whirlwind, from the hush of night, and announcing that Job, the passionate, vehement, well nigh sceptical Job, had spoken the truth; the false views of his friends were declared more offensive to heaven than Job's bitterest complaints had been.

"And it was so, that after the Lord had spoken these words unto Job, the Lord said to Eliphaz the Temanite, My wrath is kindled against thee, and against thy two friends: for ye have not spoken of me the thing that is right, as my servant Job hath. Therefore, take unto you now seven bullocks and seven rams, and go to my servant Job, and offer up for

and from the breeze of day. And doubtless the author of the Book of Job had this same experience. . . . Some persons have voices to the note of the flute, and others to the swell of the organ; but this highest reach of poetry rose to the music of the mightiest and oldest elements of nature, combining to form the various parts in the one voice of God. And how this whirlwind of poetry, once aroused, storms along! how it ruffles the foundations of the earth! how it churns up the ocean into spray! how it unveils the old treasure of the hail and the snow! how it soars up to the stars! how the lightnings say to it, 'Here we are!' how, stooping from this pitch, it sweeps over the various noble or terrible creatures of the bard's country — raising the mane of the lion, stirring the wild horror of the raven's wing, racing with the wild ass into the wilderness, flying with the eagle and the hawk, shortening speed with the lazy vastness of behemoth, awakening the thunder of the horse's neck, and daring to open 'the doors of the fire,' with the 'teeth terrible round about' of leviathan himself! The truth, the literal exactness, the freshness, fire, and rapidity of the figures presented resemble less the slow, elaborate work of a painter, than a succession of pictures taken instantaneously by the finger of the sun, and true to the smallest articulation of the burning life."

yourselves a burnt-offering; and my servant Job shall pray for you: for him will I accept: lest I deal with you after your folly, in that ye have not spoken of me the thing which is right, like my servant Job. So Eliphaz the Temanite, and Bildad the Shuhite, and Zophar the Naamathite went, and did according as the Lord commanded them: the Lord also accepted Job. And the Lord turned the captivity of Job, when he prayed for his friends: also the Lord gave Job twice as much as he had before. Then came there unto him all his brethren, and all his sisters, and all they that had been of his acquaintance before, and did eat bread with him in his house: and they bemoaned him, and comforted him over all the evil that the Lord had brought upon him: every man also gave him a piece of money, and every one an ear-ring of gold. So the Lord blessed the latter end of Job more than his beginning: for he had fourteen thousand sheep, and six thousand camels, and a thousand yoke of oxen, and a thousand she-asses. He had also seven sons and three daughters. And he called the name of the first, Jemima; and the name of the second, Kezia; and the name of the third, Keren-Happuch.* And in all the land were no women found so fair as the daughters of Job; and their father gave them inheritance among their brethren. After this lived Job a hundred and forty years, and saw his

* The names given to these daughters are suggestive. The name of the first signifies *The Day*, — a fair and elegant complexion; that of the second signifies *Cassia*, fragrant and precious; that of the third, the horn of Amalthea, "with a face splendid as the emerald."

sons, and his sons' sons, even four generations. So Job died, being old and full of days." *

This sequel is beautiful, and seemingly just as we would have it; but restorations are not always received in this life, and are but a small part of what God intends.

In that repose of one hundred and forty years Job was awaiting what eye hath not seen. He had been fitted for a sphere such as this life does not afford.

Before his trials he had been pronounced faultless in his love of God and hate of sin; afterwards he had added thereto a wealth of sanctified knowledge that made him many fold more a man. He was made fit for any service; Jehovah on the spot appointed him his arbiter and priest. (xlii. 8.) Satan had lied; he was defeated, and balked were all his wily and malignant intrigues; Job had triumphed, and became a king. No angel in heaven could have done better. Job had beaten all his enemies. Once, twice, thrice had he beaten, fairly beaten, his greatest enemy in the fray. So great was Satan's overthrow, that, in these closing scenes of the drama, he is passed over in silent contempt, and left by himself to bear the eternal disgrace of his defeat. God's confidence had not been misplaced. He was proud of his earth-born hero. God loves heroes. What honorable mention he makes of his list of worthies.† We need no longer marvel that saints are to judge the world, and rule the universe; none are fitter for *such* positions than *men* who conquer.

* Job xlii. 7-17.

† Heb. xi.

THE KING.

It is evident that there is a manifest progress in the succession of beings on the surface of the earth. This progress consists in an increasing similarity to the living fauna, and among the vertebrates, especially in their increasing resemblance to man. But this connection is not the consequence of a direct lineage between the faunas of different ages. There is nothing like parental descent connecting them. The fishes of the Palæozoic age are in no respect the ancestors of the reptiles of the Secondary age; nor does man descend from the mammals which preceded him in the Tertiary age. The link by which they are connected is of a higher and immaterial nature; and their connection is to be sought in the view of the Creator himself, whose aim in forming the earth, in allowing it to undergo the successive changes which geology has pointed out, and in creating successively all the different types of animals which have passed away, was to introduce man upon the surface of our globe. Man is the end towards which all the animal creation has tended from the first appearance of the first Palæozoic fishes. AGASSIZ.

Man was sent into the world to be a growing and exhaustless force. The world was spread out around him to be seized and conquered. Realms of infinite truth burst open above him, inviting him to tread those shining coasts along which Newton dropped his plummet, and Herschel sailed — a Columbus of the skies. CHAPIN.

I affirm, and trust that I do not speak too strongly, that there are traces of infinity in the human mind, and that, in this very respect, it bears a likeness to God. The very conception of infinity is the mark of a nature to which no limit can be prescribed. This thought, indeed, comes to us, not so much from abroad as from our own souls. We ascribe this attribute to God, because we possess capacities and wants which only an unbounded being can fill, and because we are conscious of a tendency in spiritual faculties to unlimited expansion. CHANNING.

The scrutiny of human nature on a small scale is one of the most dangerous of employments; the study of it on a large scale is one of the safest and truest. ISAAC TAYLOR.

We have more power than will; and it is often by way of excuse to ourselves that we fancy things are impossible.

ROCHEFOUCAULD.

Bounded in his nature, infinite in his desires, man is a fallen god, who has a recollection of heaven. LAMARTINE.

There is but one temple in the world, and that is the body of man. Nothing is holier than this high form. Bending before men is a reverence done to this revelation in the flesh. We touch heaven when we lay our hand on a human body.

NOVALIS.

"We touch heaven when we lay our hand on a human body!" This sounds much like a mere flourish of rhetoric; but it is not so. If well meditated, it will turn out to be a scientific fact; the expression, in such words as can be had, of the actual truth of the thing. We are the miracle of miracles — the great inscrutable mystery of God. We cannot understand it, we know not how to speak of it; but we may feel and know, if we like, that it is really so. CARLYLE.

Man is the image and glory of God. I COR. xi. 7.

He that toucheth you, toucheth the apple of his eye.

ZECH. ii. 8.

And above the firmament that was over their heads was the likeness of a throne, as the appearance of a sapphire stone, and upon the likeness of the throne was the likeness as the appearance of a man above upon it.

EZEK. i. 26.

Lord, we know what we are, but know not what we may be.

SHAKESPEARE.

THE KING.

ONE of the grandest questions now appearing in the different fields of religion, philosophy, and physical science, bears upon the relative position of humanity in the universe. Is humanity higher and essentially different from other created objects, or only upon a par with many of them, and essentially the same with all of them? Such is the question which obtrudes itself into almost every form of discussion; yet rarely has it been stated with definiteness, and still more rarely does it receive a positive and satisfactory answer.

Pantheism, whether in the form of naturalism, positivism, or poetic sentimentalism, pronounces sublimely upon the exaltation of humanity. Man, it says, is divine; he is God, therefore infinite. What more can be asked?

But pantheism has this everlasting drawback; it proves too much, and goes too far. The waxing of the dawn, the waning of the evening, the incoming tide of the sea, the jelly-fish and polype are each divine; they are God, therefore are infinite. So that the distinction and the relative pre-eminence, which the human soul feels it has an inalienable right to demand between itself and a piece of clay, is practically denied by pantheism; and hence its silence, when the idea of relative position is introduced; and hence, also, the death of speculative pantheism, anon, — for it is contrary to human conviction; it is a born and bred oddity, and odd things are not permitted to live, though supported by genius of the highest order.

Again: the philosophical and sentimental religious schemes of the day, in the various forms of liberalism, radicalism, and free inquiry, claim to place the highest possible estimate upon humanity. Advocates of these views frequently inveigh against the popular or evangelical theology, because, as they assert, it degrades humanity; making of man anything save the self-reliant son of the God, as he is according to their views. They claim, it is true, that man is his own lawgiver, judge, and final court of appeal. They give him the right to interpret for himself the truth of things, and attribute to him the power, unaided, of rising well nigh into the solitudes of the infinite.

While there may be much that is inspiring and imposing, also somewhat that is true in these conceptions, still they leave so many practical and every-day problems untouched, that we are not much better off for any instruction received therefrom. We have to blind our eyes to much voluntary wretchedness existing in humanity, or else look beyond the interpretations of liberalism. Many a *radical*, in his better moments, has confessed sad misgivings as to how the masses can be reached through *modern improvements*, and have confessed that while their machinery can take care of the refined and educated, it is not well qualified to transmute ordinary mire and clay into gods.

Five years ago, all were on tiptoe to see liberalism work out its wonderful conversions, regenerations, sanctifications, transfigurations, and flights to heaven in chariots of fire; but after all its efforts and experiments, and in spite of them, the world continues to be evangelized not one whit, save by the old instrumentalities of the popular theology, and it alone seems qualified to solve this grand problem before us.

Modern physical science is also very curious and wonderful. The data it brings us are invaluable. The amazing strides it has taken in every direction, within the last half score years, wins universal and merited applause.

But, nevertheless, some of its leading investigators come to such strange and outlandish conclusions respecting the relative attitude of man in the universe, that their announcements are forthwith vetoed by universal common sense. The tadpolean coat of arms, which certain scientists attempt to hang up in every man's house, will be turned face to the wall. We cannot, on Darwin's plan, inspire reverence for a monkey; by as much as the brute comes to look like a man is it disgusting. Humanity never has had, and never will have, stomach to bear and digest such coarse diet. In fine, humanity will always clap its hands to eyes and ears, and rightly so, whenever told that it is only a more developed polywog. Indeed, the world of science itself is rapidly receding from all such advanced views, and is slowly but surely settling back upon the everlasting foundations of revealed truth.*

* Dr. Guthrie well states in what estimate man is held by other things, and what other things do for him: —

"Infidelity regards man as little better than an animated statue, living clay, a superior animal. She sees no jewel of immortality flashing in this earthly casket. According to her, our future being is a brilliant but baseless dream of the present; death an everlasting sleep; and that dark, low, loathsome grave our eternal sepulchre.

Vice, again, looks on man as an animal formed for the indulgence of brutal appetites. She sees no divinity in his intellect, nor pure feelings, nor lofty aspirations, worthy of the cultivation for the coming state. Her foul finger never points him to the skies. She leaves powers and feelings, which might have been trained to heaven, to trail upon the ground, to be soiled and trodden in the mire, or to intwine themselves around the basest objects. In virtuous shame, in modesty, purity, integrity, gentleness, natural affection, she blights with her poisonous breath whatever vestiges of beauty have survived the Fall; and when she has done her perfect work, she leaves man a wreck, a wretch, an object of loathing, not only to God and angels, but — lowest and deepest of all degradation — an object of contempt and loathing to himself.

While infidelity regards man as a mere animal, to be dissolved at death into ashes and air, and vice changes man into a brute or devil, Mammon enslaves him. She makes him a serf, and condemns him to be a gold-digger for life in the mines. She puts her collar on his neck, and locks it; and bending his head to the soil, and bathing his brow in sweat, she says, Toil, toil, toil! as if this creature, originally made in the image of God, this dethroned and exiled monarch, to save whom the Son of God descended from the skies and bled on Calvary, were a living machine, constructed of sinew, bone and muscle, and made for no higher end than to work to live, and live to work."

Our purpose, in these leading remarks, has not been to ignore either pantheism, liberalism, or sceptical science; but merely to suggest their inadequacy at solving one of the problems most interesting to us, and to account for their comparative silence whenever questioned, and also to pave the way to the disclosures of biblical theology as to the relative position of humanity in the universe.

In the first place, there can be no controversy raised between pantheism, liberalism, or physical science on the one hand, and biblical theology on the other, as to the position man actually occupies upon this earth. They all unite in placing him upon the royal throne of this world, and place in his hands unqualifiedly the sceptre of dominion over all earth's creatures. It is an established conviction of science and philosophy, that no race of beings will ever rise, or can ever rise upon this earth, who will dare for a moment to dispute its dominion with man. In the line of physical existence it is reported from every quarter that the maximum of creation is reached; the king is found. Every branch of science, every principle of philosophy, confirm one of the first announcements of biblical theology — this: that the Almighty, in crowning man, has completed his best piece of work. From the horizontal line of the fish he has passed to the vertical column of man; mathematics can suggest nothing higher. The principle of natural selection also, so far as there is truth in it, has now fallen into the hands of a race of invincible giants; every creature bows and accepts the fiat, as God solemnly announces man's final inauguration in the sublime words,

"Have dominion over the fish of the sea, and over the fowl of the air, and over every living thing that moveth upon the earth." * Thus it remains unalterable from that day to this; six thousand years have made no change. Man, in his exaltation or humiliation, in his civilization or barbarism, is still the monarch of every inch of this earth he inhabits, and will remain thus till the end of time.

We are now prepared to seek the solution of one or two other propositions, which we do by the method of gradual approach. The intention, in a word, is to extend our inquiries from this to the heavenly or spiritual world.

The Scriptures and science agree that in the creation and fitting up of this earth the Deity has proceeded from lower to higher forms, the culmination, as we have seen, being in man. Is it not reasonable, therefore, to conclude that when the culmination is reached, the Deity will be especially inclined to embody himself in that highest form or object? It is his ideal, it is his idea; therefore is it not his especial representative? In other words, to say the least, does not the Deity show himself in that last work more than he shows himself in any other work?

But man is the completest workmanship of God on this earth; he is felt to be more God-like, more the representation or manifestation of the Deity than is anything else on earth. Man is the light of the world; he is consequently the temple of the Holy Ghost, or else there is none.

The question, then, is this; inasmuch as there has

* Gen. i. 28.

been a progressive series of creations in this world, culminating in physical humanity, which occupies the thrones of this world, why may we not draw this inference — that in the realms of the invisible universe God has also begun with lower forms of spiritual existences, and has advanced on towards higher, commencing, for instance, with spiritual polypes, and then passing on through spiritual serpents, and the different spiritual animals, the different orders of angelic existences, such as seraphs, cherubs, angels, archangels, principalities and powers, and then culminating his work in spiritual humanity, which, for a time, is placed on the thrones of the heavenly worlds, as physical humanity is placed upon the throne of the physical world? What strong confirmation does this thought receive from that marvellous statement of revelation, that "the invisible things of him, from the creation of the world, are clearly seen, being understood by the things that are made, even his eternal power and Godhead"! The correspondence between things in the physical and spiritual worlds is, by inference, undoubtedly perfect: upon entering the spiritual world we shall, in all probability, not be met by universal surprises, but with familiar forms, — of beauty in the one place, heaven; and of hideousness in the other place, hell.* So that, if the foregoing inference is

* The repeated representations of spiritual forms in heaven corresponding with the animal forms of earth (Rev. iv. 7, 8) must not have the too easy go-by, as though they meant nothing in particular. It is possible that we ought often to be a little less allegorical, and more simple, child-like and literal in our interpretation of certain scriptures. Take for

natural and true, then, by as much as physical humanity is the highest type of the physical, we may, by

illustration the temptation of Eve: the account is brief and definite. "Now the serpent was more subtle than any beast of the field which the Lord God had made: and he said unto the woman, Yea, hath God said, Ye shall not eat of every tree of the garden? And the woman said unto the serpent, We may eat of the fruit of the trees of the garden: But of the fruit of the tree which is in the midst of the garden, God hath said, Ye shall not eat of it, neither shall ye touch it, lest ye die. And the serpent said unto the woman, Ye shall not surely die: For God doth know that in the day ye eat thereof, then your eyes shall be opened; and ye shall be as gods, knowing good and evil."

The woman yielded, and then "the Lord God said unto the woman, What is this that thou hast done? And the woman said, The serpent beguiled me, and I did eat. And the Lord God said unto the serpent, Because thou hast done this, thou art cursed above all cattle, and above every beast of the field: upon thy belly shalt thou go, and dust shalt thou eat all the days of thy life: And I will put enmity between thy seed and her seed: it shall bruise thy head, and thou shalt bruise his heel." (Gen. iii. 1–5, 13–15.)

Now, what authority have we for saying this serpent was Satan? The Bible nowhere gives such authority. "Nahash," serpent or dragon, is the word employed. This account in Genesis is not allegory; it is plain, straightforward history. Why not say that it was one of the lower and fallen orders of spiritual existences, corresponding with what men in *delirium tremens* invariably see, and corresponding with the serpent species of earth which tempted Eve? To expose our first parents, being inexperienced and unsuspecting, to the temptations of the superior skill and sagacity of Satan himself, would hardly seem fitting. May we not better suppose that the agency was a serpent imp? There may be a deeper significance in the repugnance felt by man towards the ser-

analogy, argue that spiritual humanity is the highest type of the spiritual; that it is the culmination of spiritual creation, the ideal of the divine mind, the completest embodiment and representation of the divine idea, which speaks the mind and pleasure of God, which is the light of that world, the temple of the Holy Ghost there, the one which holds the sceptre and sits forever upon the throne, the brightness of God's glory and the express image of his person.*

pent tribe than appears at first upon the surface, provided it is a symbol of one of the lower orders of fallen spiritual being. (See *Outlines of Christian Theology*, p. 75.)

* Lest the point is not made clear, pardon its repetition in a little different form. God has proceeded in his creation of spiritual existences as he has in the creation of physical existences, beginning with the lower, and proceeding to the higher forms; a spiritual polypè, and then on towards a spiritual man. Quite high in this scale of spiritual existence is angelic nature, the highest type of which we may suppose to have been Satan. But angelic nature in its highest type is not the highest type that could be created. It is not the highest that God designed to create. It is not the form in which he designed to enthrone and incarnate himself. It is not the form, in fact, which he designed to place upon the universal throne, and which he was to invest with all the glory of the divine majesty; he was awaiting a still higher order of creation.

The last type and the highest type of the spiritual creation, if we mistake not, is human nature; an elder brotherhood of our humanity. The highest type of this nature God pronounced his well-beloved Son. It was so grand a display of perfected existence that God could do no more or better. He pronounced this the first born, in point of excellence, of all creation; the second personation of the eternal Godhead enthroned itself within this humanity, becoming thereby the visible Jehovah, the wielder of God's sceptre, whom Abraham

This inference may seem, for the moment, a little wild, but it certainly very closely corresponds with biblical representations. It is nowhere hinted in the Scriptures that the invisible Deity in the spiritual universe has committed the sceptre and the throne to angelic or to archangelic beings, but there are numerous representations showing that this authority has been submitted to a type of humanity.

It is also revealed that the otherwise invisible Deity enshrines himself in this highest manifestation of his creative power; and so perfect is this, his crowning work, that he is pleased to call it, not his creation, but his Son; so completely is this God's ideal, so perfect is the blending between the Father Almighty and this his chief, that they are — *one.*

In the light of this thought, the various scriptures bearing upon the subject need no interpretation; they need merely to be read. Take the opening chapter of the Bible, for instance: "Let *us* make man in our image, after our likeness." * The heavenly world must therefore have had appearances which physical humanity resembles; and not only this, but the Creator also says that it is *our* image, in which man is created.† In former times, also, as biblical theology

called "Lord," whom Manoah called "God," and who called himself "Captain of the Lord's Hosts;" and later, one with the Father Almighty: indissoluble seems to be the bond, during the present dispensation, at least; the universe has found in him its chief king, and the throne its chief occupant.

* Gen. i. 26.

† How could evil come into a pure universe? is a question attended with not a little perplexity; indeed, it is one of the

tells us, different types of this heavenly or spiritual humanity were wont to appear on the earth to patriarchs; or perhaps it would be more correct to say, that the prophetic and purified eye was enabled to see what the ordinary eye cannot see, though what was seen is likewise not far from every one of us.*

The person whom Adam met in the garden, and with whom Enoch walked, and with whom Abraham

most difficult and perplexing problems in theology. But if the supposition is correct, that Satan stood at the head of created and spiritual intelligences up to the time of the creation of pre-existent spiritual humanity, then with the introduction of this new type of creation, with a chief of whom we read, "When he bringeth in the first begotten," and saith, "Let all the angels of God worship him," it is not difficult to imagine that Lucifer, son of the morning, who had hitherto stood first, would have occasion for an inexcusable rebellion; if he rebelled, it is likely enough that a third or more would side with him. It was not the invisible God, but spiritual humanity, with which he was contending, and which he expected easily to conquer. His was the *Southern Confederacy*. He had no idea, at the outset, there would be so much blood shed, or that the campaign would last so long; but having engaged in this war, he is determined to keep it up, even in his degradation and chains. (See pages 125, 126, note.)

* Perhaps it will better harmonize with the ideas of the reader to suppose that Christ was the only type of pre-existent humanity, and that those who appeared with him were earth-born humanity: they were certainly earth-born attendants who appeared with Jesus upon the mount of transfiguration — old acquaintances, really; and so they may have been old acquaintances who appeared with Christ to Abraham. These may have been Christ's disciples in the other world — those who aforetime had gone from this world.

conversed, and with whom Jacob wrestled, and whom Moses beheld, was in each instance clothed in a human form. The passages recounting these things are perfectly simple, if we look at them as we should — that is, with child-like simplicity; but they are perfectly amazing if we look at them in any other light. What, for illustration, is the obvious interpretation of the following account?

"And the Lord appeared unto him (Abraham) in the plains of Mamre; and he sat in the tent-door in the heat of the day; and he lifted up his eyes and looked, and lo, three men stood by him." The account then states that Abraham entertained them; and after the entertainment we read, "And the men rose up from thence, and looked toward Sodom; and Abraham went with them to bring them on their way. And the Lord said, Shall I hide from Abraham that thing which I do?"

We next read that this Lord, who was one of the three men, made the following disclosure: "And the Lord said, Because the cry of Sodom and Gomorrah is great, and because their sin is very grievous, I will go down now,"—that is, they were on the table lands above those cities, — "and see whether they have done altogether according to the cry of it which is come unto me; and if not, I will know. And the men" — two of the three — "turned their faces from thence, and went toward Sodom; but Abraham stood yet before the Lord."

Then followed the intercessions of Abraham in behalf of the city: —

"And Abraham drew near, and said, Wilt thou

also destroy the righteous with the wicked? Peradventure there be fifty righteous within the city: wilt thou also destroy and not spare the place for the fifty righteous that are therein? That be far from thee to do after this manner, to slay the righteous with the wicked; and that the righteous should be as the wicked, that be far from thee: Shall not the Judge of all the earth do right? And the Lord said, If I find in Sodom fifty righteous within the city, then I will spare all the place for their sakes. And Abraham answered and said, Behold now I have taken upon me to speak unto the Lord, which am but dust and ashes. Peradventure there shall lack five of the fifty righteous: wilt thou destroy all the city for lack of five? And he said, If I find there forty and five, I will not destroy it. And he spake unto him yet again, and said, Peradventure there shall be forty found there. And he said, I will not do it for forty's sake. And he said unto him, O, let not the Lord be angry, and I will speak: Peradventure there shall thirty be found there. And he said, I will not do it, if I find thirty there. And he said, Behold now I have taken upon me to speak unto the Lord: Peradventure there shall be twenty found there. And he said, I will not destroy it for twenty's sake. And he said, O, let not the Lord be angry, and I will speak yet but this once. Peradventure ten shall be found there. And he said, I will not destroy it for ten's sake. And the Lord went his way as soon as he had left communing with Abraham: and Abraham returned unto his place." *

* Gen. xviii.

Whatever our notions of this interview may be, this is true: that the strange being, who looked, so far as Abraham could see, like a man, who had companions with him, who could read the hearts of the men of Sodom, and who could destroy their city, talked as though he was man, and as though he was God. But without anticipating too much, we may refer to another instance.

Just before the overthrow of Jericho, Joshua, while reconnoitring, saw a man with a drawn sword. So thoroughly real and human was this man, that Joshua challenged him, to know to which side he belonged. "As captain of the Lord's hosts am I come," he replied. In the same sentence, that strange visitant was called, "man," "Jehovah," and the "captain of the Lord's hosts."

This scene is also in perfect keeping with the visit made to the parents of Samson. The one who stood before them looked like a man, they called him a man, they spoke to him as to a man; but his words and his works were so wonderful, that when he departed, "Manoah said unto his wife, We shall surely die, because we have seen God. But his wife said unto him, If the Lord were pleased to kill us, he would not have showed us all these things."

In addition to these appearances of spiritual humanity on the earth, another fact is worthy of mention: the prophetic eye and inspired heart have been permitted, at different times, to look in upon the spiritual world; but they have made only one discovery, and have returned only one report bearing upon the thought before us; they have seen, from first to last, a type of humanity of the most dazzling brightness, occupying the throne of the invisible God, and holding the sceptre of supreme authority; the glory of God and a human face are the almost invariable association. "And above the firmament that was over their heads was the likeness of a throne, as the appearance of a sapphire stone: and upon the likeness of the throne was the likeness as the appearance of a man above upon it," * is a characteristic representation. When Stephen stood before his bloodthirsty persecutors, he said, "Behold, I see the heavens opened, and the Son of man standing on the right hand of God." †

Throughout those marvellous visions of the Apocalypse also, the reigning glory of the Infinite One uniformly finds its embodiment in a human face and human form.

Indirect confirmation of all this is found, likewise, in the inspired statements of the apostle Paul: "For unto which of the angels said he at any time, Thou art my son; this day have I begotten thee"? "And again, when he bringeth in the first begotten into the world, he saith, And let all the angels of God worship him." "Unto the Son he saith, Thy throne, O God, is forever and ever; a sceptre of righteousness is the sceptre of thy kingdom." ‡

But, is it asked, has the invisible and infinite God a human form? Nay, not as one might infer, perhaps; but, nevertheless, he that sits upon the throne of God has a form, and that form is like the form of a man —

* Ezek. i. 26. † Acts vii. 56. ‡ Heb. i. 5, vi. 8.

it is the form of a man. And when we enter the spiritual and heavenly world, and are thrilled by the ineffable glory of God, and look to behold the grandeur of his throne, before which all the nations are gathered, we shall see seated upon it — *man.**

We have reached this conclusion, then: that not only is the place of supreme authority on the earth occupied by humanity, but also the place of supreme authority in the heavenly world, at least according to the Scriptures, is also occupied by humanity — that is, by spiritual humanity.

Before we can correctly infer the future relative position of our humanity, as now met with in this earth, namely, fallen humanity, it becomes necessary to introduce more positively a connecting link, known, in technical language, as Christology.

At the outset, we find the heavenly throne occupied by a type of humanity. The Scriptures leave no doubt but that the one in whom the second person of the Trinity — the *Logos* element or capacity, from first to last (alpha and omega) — embodies himself, is identical with the Lord who appeared and talked with Abraham, and also identical with that being whom we call Jesus, who appeared in Judea eighteen hundred years ago, with this difference: that the spiritual

* Does this thought suggest to any mind the idea of humiliation on the part of God? But the objection is universal, and involves too much; for whenever and wherever the infinite touches the finite, there is scientific humiliation, be it in the fashioning of lilies, the creation of worlds, the redemption of man, or the occupancy of a throne in this or in the heavenly world.

humanity of this Wonderful One came into possession of physical humanity through Mary, his mother, *somehow*.

Is this perfectly bewildering? Perhaps so.

But the point of identity need not be perfectly bewildering, if at least we are willing to rely upon biblical fact and history.

Late in December, and during his early Judean ministry, *our Lord* crossed the rich plains to the south of Ebal and Gerizim, and rested on the broad curb of a well known as Jacob's. He was hungry and athirst. Memorable was the conversation that followed between himself and the woman of Samaria.*

But nearly two thousand years before, during the heat of a midsummer's day, by the oaks of Mamre *the Lord* appeared, as a man to a man, and held familiar intercourse with Abraham. The words spoken and the acts performed were as human as were those at the well of Samaria. And Abraham said, "My Lord, if now I have found favor in thy sight, pass not away, I pray thee, from thy servant: Let a little water, I pray you, be fetched, and wash your feet, and rest yourselves under the tree: And I will fetch a morsel of bread, and comfort ye your hearts; after that ye shall pass on; for therefore are ye come to your servant. And they said, So do, as thou hast said. And Abraham hastened into the tent unto Sarah, and said, Make ready quickly three measures of fine meal, knead it, and make cakes upon the hearth. And Abraham ran unto the herd, and fetched a calf,

* John iv.

tender and good, and gave it unto a young man; and he hasted to dress it. And he took butter, and milk, and the calf which he had dressed, and set it before them; and he stood by them under the tree, and they did eat."*

During our Lord's ministry in Northern Galilee, upon the eve of a day in the month of April, he sent his disciples across the Sea of Tiberias. The fourth watch should have found them safely on the opposite shore; but the waves were angry, and the winds tempestuous; in consequence, they were still toiling in mid sea. "And," we read, "he saw them toiling in rowing; for the wind was contrary unto them: and about the fourth watch of the night he cometh unto them, walking upon the sea, and would have passed by them. But when they saw him walking upon the sea, they supposed it had been a spirit, and cried out. (For they all saw him, and were troubled.) And immediately he talked with them, and saith unto them, Be of good cheer: it is I; be not afraid. And Peter answered him, and said, Lord, if it be thou, bid me come unto thee on the water. And he said, Come. And when Peter was come down out of the ship, he walked on the water to go to Jesus. But when he saw the wind boisterous, he was afraid; and beginning to sink, he cried, saying, Lord, save me. And immediately Jesus stretched forth his hand, and caught him, and said unto him, O thou of little faith, wherefore didst thou doubt? And he went up unto them into the ship; and the wind ceased; and they

* Gen. xviii. 2–8.

were sore amazed in themselves beyond measure, and wondered. For they considered not the miracle of the loaves; for their heart was hardened. And when they had passed over, they came into the land of Gennesaret, and drew to the shore. Then they that were in the ship came and worshipped him, saying, Of a truth thou art *the Son of God*."*

But, six hundred years before the Christian era, Nebuchadnezzar, the greatest and most powerful of the kings of Babylon, in a fit of violence and fury, heated to seven times its wont his furnace, and, while its fires were raging and roaring as the waves of the sea, he cast therein three worthy children of God. The king looked. The record describes the rest.

"Then Nebuchadnezzar the king was astonished, and rose up in haste, and spake, and said unto his counsellors, Did not we cast three men bound into the midst of the fire? They answered and said unto the king, True, O king. He answered and said, Lo, I see four men loose, walking in the midst of the fire, and they have no hurt; and the form of the fourth is like *the Son of God*.†

It was also during this ministry in Northern Galilee, either for the sake of security or seclusion, that our Lord passed for a time into the confines of Tyre. While there he was met by a poor woman, who accosted him with words that sound strange enough on heathen lips: "Have mercy on me, Lord, thou Son of David; my daughter is grievously vexed with a devil." Passionate was her appeal. In her agony

* Mark vi. 48-53. Matt. xiv. 28-31.

† Dan. iii. 24, 25.

and importunity, she wrestled as if of giant's strength with one she could not appear to move. Seemingly too long was that night of supplicating entreaty. But in the morning of her deliverance we hear the Master say, "O woman, great is thy faith: be it unto thee even as thou wilt. And her daughter was made whole from that very hour." * "And when she was come to her house, she found the devil gone out, and her daughter laid upon the bed." †

But, many centuries before this triumph of the Syro-Phenician (princess) woman, was another conquest, which, in many respects, is not much unlike it.

A small stream, rising near Rabbath Ammon, flowing into the Jordan, and separating North Gilead from South, or the kingdom of Og from that of Sihon, was known as the brook Jabbok. Over this, at nightfall, Jacob, staff in hand, passed into the silence and loneliness beyond. There he was met by a *man*. Literal and typical both was that night-long struggle. The patriarch felt that he was in the presence of a power that could bless or curse. "Let me go," said the mighty stranger, "for the dawn ariseth." But Jacob, though disabled, still clung to his conqueror, and replied, "I will not let thee go except thou bless me." The stranger said unto Jacob, "What is thy name? And he said, Jacob. And he said, Thy name shall be called no more Jacob, but Israel: for as a prince hast thou power with God, and with men, and hast prevailed. And Jacob asked him, and said, Tell me, I pray thee, thy name: and he said, Wherefore is it that thou dost ask after my name? And he blessed

* Matt. xv. 28. † Mark vii. 30.

him there. And Jacob called the name of the place Peniel: for I have seen God face to face, and my life is preserved." *

Is not the marked correspondence between this Lord

* Gen. xxxii. 27-30.

Note further parallelisms in the following passages: —

"And on the morrow, when they were come from Bethany, he was hungry. And seeing a fig tree afar off, having leaves, he came, if haply he might find anything thereon: and when he came to it, he found nothing but leaves: for the time of figs was not yet. And Jesus answered and said unto it, No man eat fruit of thee hereafter forever. And his disciples heard it." Mark xi. 12-14.

"And presently the fig tree withered away." Matt. xxi. 19.

"And the Lord said, Because the cry of Sodom and Gomorrah is great, and because their sin is very grievous, I will go down now, and see whether they have done altogether according to the cry of it, which is come unto me; and if not, I will know." Gen. xviii. 20, 21.

"Then the Lord rained upon Sodom and upon Gomorrah brimstone and fire from the Lord out of heaven; and he overthrew those cities and all the plain, and all the inhabitants of the cities, and that which grew upon the ground." Gen. xix. 24, 25.

"Then said Jesus unto them again, Verily, verily, I say unto you, I am the door of the sheep. All that ever came before me are thieves and robbers: but the sheep did not hear them. I am the door: by me if any man enter in, he shall be saved, and shall go in and out, and find pasture. The thief cometh not, but for to steal, and to kill, and to destroy: I am come that they might have life, and that they might have it more abundantly. I am the good shepherd: the good shepherd giveth his life for the sheep. But he that is a hireling, and not the shepherd, whose own the sheep are not,

of the Old Testament and Jesus of the New, even upon this hasty review, very surprising? Transpose the historic relations and they will each fill the place

seeth the wolf coming, and leaveth the sheep, and fleeth; and the wolf catcheth them, and scattereth the sheep. The hireling fleeth, because he is a hireling, and careth not for the sheep. I am the good shepherd, and know my sheep, and am known of mine." John x. 7–14.

"Behold, I send an angel before thee, to keep thee in the way, and to bring thee into the place which I have prepared. Beware of him, and obey his voice; provoke him not, for he will not pardon your transgressions: for my name is in him. But if thou shalt indeed obey his voice, and do all that I speak, then I will be an enemy unto thine enemies, and an adversary unto thine adversaries. For mine angel shall go before thee, and bring thee in unto the Amorites, and the Hittites, and the Perizzites, and the Canaanites, and the Hivites, and the Jebusites; and I will cut them off. Thou shalt not bow down to their gods, nor serve them, nor do after their works; but thou shalt utterly overthrow them, and quite break down their images. And ye shall serve the Lord your God, and he shall bless thy bread, and thy water; and I will take sickness away from the midst of thee." Exodus xxiii. 20–25.

"Then they went out to see what was done; and came to Jesus, and found the man out of whom the devils were departed, sitting at the feet of Jesus, clothed, and in his right mind: and they were afraid. They also which saw it told them by what means he that was possessed of the devils was healed. Then the whole multitude of the country of the Gadarenes round about besought him to depart from them; for they were taken with great fear." Luke viii. 35–37.

"In the year that king Uzziah died, I saw also the Lord sitting upon a throne, high and lifted up, and his train filled

of the other. They both appeared in the form of humanity. They both left the glory of heaven to instruct, encourage, and save mankind. They both acted the part of mediator. They both received divine hon-

the temple. Above it stood the seraphims: each one had six wings; with twain he covered his face, and with twain he covered his feet, and with twain he did fly. And one cried unto another, and said, Holy, holy, holy, is the Lord of hosts: the whole earth is full of his glory. And the posts of the door moved at the voice of him that cried, and the house was filled with smoke. Then said I, Woe is me! for I am undone; because I am a man of unclean lips, and I dwell in the midst of a people of unclean lips: for mine eyes have seen the King, the Lord of hosts." Is. vi. 1–5.

"And it came to pass, about eight days after these sayings, he took Peter, and John, and James, and went up into a mountain to pray. And as he prayed, the fashion of his countenance was altered, and his raiment was white and glistering. And behold, there talked with him two men, which were Moses and Elias, who appeared in glory, and spake of his decease, which he should accomplish at Jerusalem. But Peter and they that were with him were heavy with sleep: and when they were awake, they saw his glory, and the two men that stood with him. And it came to pass, as they departed from him, Peter said unto Jesus, Master, it is good for us to be here: and let us make three tabernacles; one for thee, and one for Moses, and one for Elias: not knowing what he said. While he thus spake, there came a cloud, and overshadowed them: and they feared as they entered into the cloud. And there came a voice out of the cloud, saying, This is my beloved Son: hear him. And when the voice was past, Jesus was found alone. And they kept it close, and told no man in those days any of those things which they had seen." Luke ix. 28–36.

"Then went up Moses and Aaron, Nadab, and Abihu, and seventy of the elders of Israel: And they saw the God of

ors, performed divine acts, and spoke as only God has a right to speak.* Indeed, do they not seem to be the same essentially? † Paul we find distinctly declaring that they are identical.

Israel: and there was under his feet as it were a paved work of a sapphire stone, and as it were the body of heaven in his clearness. And upon the nobles of the children of Israel he laid not his hand: also they saw God, and did eat and drink. And the Lord said unto Moses, Come up to me into the mount, and be there: and I will give thee tables of stone, and a law, and commandments which I have written; that thou mayest teach them. And Moses rose up, and his minister Joshua; and Moses went up into the mount of God. And he said unto the elders, Tarry ye here for us until we come again unto you; and, behold, Aaron and Hur are with you: if any man have any matters to do, let him come unto them. And Moses went up into the mount, and a cloud covered the mount. And the glory of the Lord abode upon Mount Sinai, and the cloud covered it six days: and the seventh day he called unto Moses out of the midst of the cloud. And the sight of the glory of the Lord was like devouring fire on the top of the mount in the eyes of the children of Israel. And Moses went into the midst of the cloud, and gat him up into the mount: and Moses was in the mount forty days and forty nights. Ex. xxiv. 9–18.

* Outlines of Christian Theology.

† We say *essentially*, because there were differences growing out of the nature of the case. The embodiment in the one case was spiritual, in the other case physical: the one condition could have felt nothing of the tendency given to the race in the transgression of Adam; the other condition connected with a body from a mother belonging to the fallen race, though probably among the purest and most perfect of all women, would seem to have been to some extent affected thereby. But that they are *essentially* the same is supported by the strongest evidence.

"Moreover, brethren, I would not that ye should be ignorant how that all our fathers were under the cloud, and all passed through the sea; and did all drink the same spiritual drink; for they drank of that spiritual rock that followed them; and that rock was Christ." *

Figurative, does some one say? Nay, why not real? for so our blessed Lord interpreted it. "Abraham rejoiced to see my day, and saw it;" saw it two thousand years before the words were spoken in Judea; saw it when he ate and drank with the God-man under the oaks of Mamre.

But beyond all cavil are the explicit announcements of our Lord himself, that he was actually, personally, and consciously this Old Testament Jehovah, whose home was in heaven long before he came as the son of Mary. "These words spake Jesus, and lifted up his eyes to heaven, and said, Father, the hour is come; glorify thy Son, that thy Son also may glorify thee: As thou hast given him power over all flesh, that he should give eternal life to as many as thou hast given him. And this is life eternal, that they might know thee the only true God, and Jesus Christ whom thou hast sent. I have glorified thee on the earth, I have finished the work which thou gavest me to do. And now, O Father, glorify thou me with thine own self, with the glory which I had with thee before the world was." †

Does not this language show that Jesus Christ, as humanity, had an existence before he appeared upon the hills of Galilee or on the plains of Judea? Could

* 1 Cor. x. 1–4. † John xvii. 1–5.

the deity of Christ have offered that prayer? Must it not have been, in all fair interpretation, none other than the pre-existent humanity of Christ, which said, "Glorify thou me with thine own self, with the glory which I had with thee before the world was"? Upon that supposition all difficulties vanish; on any other supposition are they not greatly multiplied?

Note also, as further evidence, the reply of Jesus to Nicodemus. "Verily, verily, I say unto thee, We speak that we do know, and testify that we have seen; and ye receive not our witness. If I have told you earthly things, and ye believe not, how shall ye believe if I tell you of heavenly things? And no man hath ascended up to heaven, but he that came down from heaven, even the Son of man which is in heaven." *

Upon this passage we can do no better than quote the comment of Deán Alford: "All attempts to explain away the plain sense of this verse are futile and ridiculous. The Son of man, the Lord Jesus, the Word made flesh, *was in*, *came down from*, and *was in heaven while here*, and ascended up into heaven when he left this earth."

Similar to this, also, is our Saviour's address to his wavering disciples, upon a certain occasion when many were leaving him. "Many, therefore, of his disciples, when they had heard this, said, This is a hard saying: who can hear it? When Jesus knew in himself that his disciples murmured at it, he said unto them, Doth this offend you? What and if ye shall see the Son of man ascend up where he was before?"

* John iii. 11-13. Note in this connection Deut. xxx. 4, xxx. 12, Rom. x. 6-8.

Notice the language: "*What and if ye shall see the Son of man ascend up where he was before.*" Can human speech be more exact? But we must pause, as there seems to be no end to these wonderful confirmations and correspondences; in a word, the parallels run along respecting this chief of humanity in the Old Testament and in the New, the parallelism growing more and more striking, until it becomes, in the Lord Jesus, *conscious identity;* and, accordingly, Jesus has thus expressed himself. His words upon this point are certainly more authoritative than the indefinite and misty generalizations of either extreme conservatism or extreme radicalism.

We have, therefore, the direct statements of Christ, and other explicit announcements of revelation, together with Old Testament representations, and also the harmony and consistency of things, uniting in the assurance that the Son, in whom the Godhead dwelt, and who has been the glory of God for the past eighteen hundred years, was also the glory of God in heaven long before he appeared upon the hills of Galilee and plains of Judea. He is now the glory of God more than ever before; * so much so, that God, with

* This is certainly a natural inference. For Christ, both in his pre-existent and in his historic life, was the image of God, the only special and personal image God has given the universe, except that we are fashioned after the same likeness. When, in that anti-physical period of the universe, the Creator had reached this his appropriate tabernacle, the one embodying every imaginable perfection of spiritual creation, the true King of the universe, the vicegerent of God in both the spiritual and physical worlds, whose identity in both worlds is consciously, and in consequence essentially, the

all his rights and titles, has transferred himself into this one; and he it is who has arisen from the dead, and ascended to heaven; and whatever be the changes and transformations of the universe hereafter, he it is who will occupy the throne forever.

And more than this, through his resurrection and exaltation all humanity, who will consent, and who will accept him, are also lifted into these same exalted rela-

same, it was pre-eminently fitting that Deity should embody and enthrone itself therein. When this divine representative came to the earth, taking a physical body, with more or less of the pure physical human nature from Mary his mother, he lost nothing in nature, though something in circumstance, but gained much in character. Here was a humiliation involving advancement. Here was a humiliation of the indwelling Deity, it is true, but the spiritual tabernacle in which the Deity had pre-existed was exalted, on the other hand, by that connection with physical humanity; and no less, but more glorious will Christ appear, throughout eternity, on account of that connection. (Compare Heb. ii. 10; v. 8, 9.) In harmony with this are the usual methods of divine procedure. The case stands thus: Human physical nature, being created later than spiritual human nature, is greater than spiritual human nature; though spiritualized human nature may, in the future transformations, be higher still; so, at least, we should naturally infer, for science informs us that the latest of a given type in the order of creation is the highest.

But more than this: the humanity of this earth-born King we have seen, is not eternal, but the spirit that dwelt within him is eternal, because it is God. The humanity of the spiritual and heavenly born King, we may likewise infer, was not eternal; but the spirit that dwelt within him was eternal, because it was God. The right of this one of Nazareth to occupy the throne of humanity has, in time past, been disputed. Certain infidels, the world over and history through, have

tions with himself. "For we are made partakers of Christ."* "If children, then heirs, heirs of God and joint heirs with Christ."† "It doth not yet appear what we shall be, but we know that when he shall appear we shall be like him;‡ and that is enough.

We are now prepared to support the well nigh startling revelation of biblical theology already hinted: that fallen humanity, possessing the spirit of this exalted chief, is with him enthroned for the judgment and government of this universe; or, in other words, fallen humanity in Christ is eternal and universal King. Our final appeal, in the settlement of all these grandest of questions, must of necessity be the holy and inspired Scriptures.

There is but a single original passage which seems to oppose the view that humanity is the highest order of created intelligence, and therefore, by nature and by right, qualified to be inaugurated as king. In the Psalms we read, "When I consider thy heavens, the work of thy fingers, the moon and the stars, which thou hast ordained, what is man, that thou art mindful of him? and the son of man, that thou visitest him? For thou hast made him a little lower than the angels, and hast crowned him with glory and

contested his right to wield the sceptre; but he holds it still. The noblest and the best men of all times have been his supporters: the throne of Jesus Christ is now firmly established in this world so long as it shall stand. So Satan disputed his right to the throne long ages since; but dismal is the doom of all, first and last, who contend with the *Son.*

* Heb. iii. 14. † Rom. viii. 17.

‡ 1 John iii. 2.

honor. Thou madest him to have dominion over the works of thy hands; thou hast put all things under his feet: all sheep and oxen, yea, and the beasts of the field, the fowl of the air, and the fish of the sea, and whatsoever passeth through the paths of the seas.* This passage calls attention to two things: the starry heavens above man, and the majesty of humanity within man. But the force of the original is not quite disclosed in the common translation.

The word here translated "angels," a little lower than "angels," is "*eloheim*," which means God; the great Hebrew scholar Gesenius accordingly translates the passage thus: "For thou hast caused him to lack but little of (a) God." A literal translation likewise is the following: "What is man! and thou art mindful of him; and the child of man! thou visitest him, and hast created him but a shaving from Deity." So that this passage, upon the highest authority, turns out in support of the merited exaltation of humanity.

But apart from this, the passages which directly declare that man, in his redeemed state, stands high above all created objects and beings in the universe, are both numerous and definite.

First, taking Jesus of Nazareth as the representative, we read, "God, who at sundry times and in divers manners spake in time past unto the fathers by the prophets, hath in these last days spoken unto us by his Son, whom he hath appointed heir of all things, by whom also he made the worlds; who being the brightness of his glory, and the express image of his

* Ps. viii. 3–8. Comp. Heb. ii. 6–9.

person, and upholding all things by the word of his power, when he had by himself purged our sins, sat down on the right hand of the Majesty on high; being made so much better than the angels, as he hath by inheritance obtained a more excellent name than they." *

Next, of those who have partaken of his nature, we read, "Know ye not that your bodies are the members of Christ?" † "What! know ye not that your body is the temple of the Holy Ghost which is in you?" ‡ "He that believeth on me, the works that I do shall he do also; and greater works than these shall he do." § "And I appoint unto you a kingdom, as my Father hath appointed unto me, that ye may eat and drink at my table, in my kingdom, and sit on thrones judging the twelve tribes of Israel." ‖

"And I saw thrones," says the Revelator, "and the saints of God sat upon them, and judgment was given unto them." ¶ "Do ye not know that the saints shall judge the world? and if the world shall be judged by you, are ye unworthy to judge the smallest matters?" ** "Know ye not that ye shall judge angels?" ††

It is clear, therefore, according to biblical theology, that God is to share his chief glories, not with angels or archangels, but with men who prove themselves worthy. In humanity are found the sole heirs with Christ of this universe. It is humanity, and nothing

* Heb. i. 1-4. † 1 Cor. vi. 15. ‡ 1 Cor. vi. 19.
§ John xiv. 12. ‖ Matt. xix. 28. ¶ Rev. xx. 4.
** 1 Cor. vi. 2. †† 1 Cor. vi. 3.

else, that has the grandest coat of arms worn in God's great empire — a coat of arms that need not be turned face to the wall, only as we, by a sinful life, disgrace our high ancestry. Man is kith and kin of the King Supreme. His is not patented, but is blood nobility. How noble-like and prince-like he ought to deport himself! The blood that is in the veins of the Lord Most High is in our veins; it is human blood; we are of one and the same family. No wonder that "he that hath the seven spirits of God, and the seven stars," after scanning the grandeurs and sublimities of things to us invisible, implored the church in Philadelphia to remain steadfast: "hold that fast which thou hast, *that no man take thy crown.*" * No wonder that, when God announces that *a man is born*, the angels pause in adoration and amazement. And no wonder that, when God announces that *a man is born again*, the angels break their silence, and fill heaven with glad and triumphal shouts.† Yes, everything, even angels, tell us that it is humanity which stands next to God, with nothing between; it well nigh stands for God. "Ye are the light of the world." It is man for whom there is such intense anxiety in heaven. For man all the angels of God are ministering spirits, sent forth to minister to the heirs of salvation. And do not our own soul convictions, which, in our better moments, take possession of us, harmonize with these daring representations? Does not every man feel that there is nothing which can intervene between him and the Infinite? Are we not each

* Rev. iii. 1, 7, 11. † Luke xv. 10.

"persuaded, that neither death, nor life, nor angels, nor principalities, nor powers, nor things present, nor things to come, nor height, nor depth, nor any other creature, shall be able to separate us from the love of God which is in Christ Jesus our Lord"?* If defeated, we are our own defeaters.

Who is this great giant spirit of evil that sometimes flashes through the world, going about seeking whom he may devour, which we call the devil? But the weakest child of humanity can resist and conquer him, and put him into terrible confusion and flight.

Or does liberalism insinuate that biblical theology places low estimates upon the power and majesty of humanity? We beg pardon, if there is anything to beg pardon for, but so-called free religion has not yet begun to dream of the exaltation of humanity as revealed in the Scriptures, and never will be able to realize it, until the light of Christianity shall be permitted to aid in its investigations.

True it is, almost while we are in the act of thinking of such exaltation and pre-eminence for humanity, that confusion and seeming discrepancy meet us. The image is blurred. Total depravity flaunts itself before us. Some poor sot, some wretch of earth, violent and fiendish, confronts us, and we ask, Is this — this *thing* — the son of a king, the heir apparent of a throne?

But hold! *that* is not humanity; that is a wreck of humanity. We always say of such, His humanity is gone. And yet, even in that wreck is royal blood;

* Rom. viii. 38, 39.

he is a prince, notwithstanding his fall; to him can the line of undisputed royalty be traced; so grand is he, even in his degradation, that his brother king left heaven to die for his restoration; and God is willing to do anything to save him.

The ignorance of humanity likewise aggravates and disappoints us. When we see parents murdering their children to propitiate the most ill-shapen images; when we see men worshipping, not God, but an ox, nay, the image of an ox; trembling, not before the great potentates of the world, but before a dog or a cat, and adoring deified garlic and onions, we almost loathe the race to which we belong. But there is more in all this than appears upon the surface. Those devotees look beyond the image, the ox, and the garlic; they are inspired and terrified by invisible agencies. It is not what those men have not attained to, but what they are capable of attaining, that should impress us, and fill us too, with awe and reverence.

The crimes of humanity in civilized lands are likewise appalling. How ungodlike they are! Men are fired with ambition, and allow nothing to stand in their way; they regard not man, and fear not God. But this aspiring soul which is "insolvent, and cannot satisfy its own wants;" * which sees no station in life too high for its occupancy; which feels an unholy pang whenever another holds a position higher than its own; which "storms heaven itself in its folly;" † which cannot see a sovereign without longing to be itself a sovereign, and sit umpire of the universe, — bespeaks for itself no grovelling, but lofty relationships.

* Emerson. † Horace.

"Ambition," says Montaigne, "is not a vice of little people." What mean these sudden flashes of ambitious graspings for positions and authority, unless they disclose the outlines of a soul towering enough, if sanctified, to be a second God in the universe?

Men likewise, while harboring revenge, commit wild and unsanctified deeds. Transgression, based upon revenge, is characteristic; there is something contradictory in it. Bruyère is right in saying, "It is thorough madness that we hate an enemy, and think of revenging ourselves; and it is thorough indolence that we are appeased, and do not revenge ourselves." Revenge is as insatiable as the grave. "Had all his hairs been lives, my great revenge had stomach for them all."* It is likewise deliberate when deepest. There is nothing heated, and nothing hasty. The violence of revenge is a cold and deliberative violence. It is madness, but a madness full of method. Such a man's sleep is but the lull between storms. For twenty years will a revengeful man pursue the object of his hate; never daunted, he will follow on, and on, until he faces his victim. When that hour comes, he will be in transports of malice; he will impersonate revenge; he will hesitate for a moment, as if it were too great a luxury to strike just yet; he will torture his victim, and sip his sweet cup. He smiles as he smites. So long as the agonies of death can be traced in the victim, he is happy.

But when they have ceased, and his fiendish life-work is done, then all things change. Through life

* Shakespeare.

the murderer had been developing unconsciously a sense of justice, a keen sense of justice, destitute of mercy. "Revenge," says Bacon, "is a kind of wild justice." And now this terrible justice, both wild and sensitive, reacts; conscience becomes a pursuer, and the fires of hell burn so deep in that man's soul, that the appalling tragedy of his life ends only when his own life ends by the same hand that slew his foe.

We see here, it is true, fiendish malignity; but it is, nevertheless, the perversion of an ennobling sentiment, inherent in the soul of man. Sin, of all kinds, is, in fact, only the wreck of sublime virtues; but it is an appalling wreck; the revengeful character, if not perverted, and if sanctified, would represent just resentment, to what is wrong, and a holy indignation against unrighteousness. Like the sword of justice, keen, but innocent and righteous, it would glisten only when espousing God's honor. It would be capable of announcing Jehovah's judgments, and could execute, with its own right arm, the sublimest behests of the Infinite One.

No less awful is rebellion in the heart of man — that power which can say "No" to God's "Yes;" which can curse God, though dying in the act. See! there is a man who has but five minutes to live. God says, "Give me thy heart." He replies, "I will not."

What! what is this, which, amid such appalling scenes, can resist angels, principalities, powers, things present, and things to come, and God himself? What is this which can defy chains, and racks, and gibbets, and fires, and all the powers of universal nature? What art thou, immortal and invisible spirit, unless thou art — a God in ruins!

Providence, too, is, or appears to be, singular in its assignments, if men are God's sons. She often puts them to employments that seem, at least, ill befitting to princes. They rarely are found in regal palaces, but are often seen tilling the soil, with brow not crowned with diamonds, but beaded with sweat and dust. They are seen plying the needle, with weary fingers and broken hearts; are found toiling down in coal-pits, and, with grimy face and besmeared hands, are for years assigned the task of firing and driving the locomotive along dusty railways, in actual peril, and near possible death every day and every hour.

Is not all this evidence of humiliation, rather than exaltation? True; so it seems, at least; but remember the chief Prince himself touched the earth to rise again. Kings may be born in stables without prejudicing in the least their titles.* In that act of tilling

* "Oftentimes, at Oxford," says De Quincey, "I saw Levana in my dreams. I knew her by her Roman symbols. Who is Levana? Reader, that do not pretend to have leisure for very much scholarship, you will not be angry with me for telling you Levana was the Roman goddess that performed for the new-born infant the earliest office of ennobling kindness, — typical, by its mode, of that grandeur which belongs to man everywhere, and of that benignity in powers invisible, which, even in pagan worlds, sometimes descends to sustain it. At the very moment of birth, just as the infant tasted for the first time the atmosphere of our troubled planet, it was laid on the ground. *That* might bear different interpretations. But immediately, lest so grand a creature should grovel there for more than one instant, either the paternal hand, as proxy for the goddess Levana, or some near kinsman, as proxy for the father, raised it upright, bade it look erect, as the king of all this world, and presented its fore-

the soil may be involved the preliminaries of future inauguration, if the work is faithfully done; the coal-pit worker may be unconsciously furnishing supplies to light the Lord's house, upon the occasion of receiving the throne and sceptre. No matter about the kind of work; how the work is done decides its merit.

The poor woman who stitches her life into her work at midnight may be finishing a robe for herself so royal that no other fingers are fit to touch it, lest it be soiled.

Surely our employments do not change our blood relations, and, through their tasks and daily work, whatever its character, and through all sorts of losses and temporary defeats, these royal sons of God will yet carve their way to thrones and empires. And often, very often, does not this princely character of man crop out, almost in spite of itself, even in the humblest avocations?

John Manyard, a pilot on one of the fated steamers of Lake Erie, toiling summer and winter, and exposed to all weathers, scarcely seemed engaged in princely employment. But on board that steamer one day was heard the cry of fire; the flames broke out amidships; the captain gave command to head for the shore; the passengers rushed to the prow of the boat; John Manyard was at the wheel; the flames and smoke became

head to the stars, saying, perhaps, in his heart, 'Behold what is greater than yourselves!' This symbolic act represented the function of Levana. And that mysterious lady, who never revealed her face (except to me in dreams), but always acted by delegation, had her name from the Latin verb (as still it is the Italian verb), *levare*, to raise aloft."

suffocating, driving him from the wheel-house farther astern; there he adjusted the spare tiller, keeping the boat meantime headed for the shore; the lives of all on board were in the hands of that rough, copper-faced man at the helm. Ten minutes! If the boat could be kept headed for the shore, they were all that was needed to save every imperilled life.

"John Manyard!" shouted the captain.

"Ay, ay, sir," was the reply.

"Can you keep her headed as she is for ten minutes?"

"I'll try, sir."

But every minute the flames and smoke increased, every minute saw the flames creeping onward towards this faithful pilot.

"John Manyard!" again shouted the captain. Every ear was strained, and caught the stifled —

"Ay, ay, sir."

"Can you keep her headed as she is for five minutes?"

And the quick ear of the captain just caught the response through the roaring flames, —

"I'll try, sir."

That was enough. The boat sped on. She veered not one inch from her course. A few fathoms more — the distance is passed; the keel grates; the shore is reached; not one life is lost, — save that of the pilot, who was found burned to a crisp, but holding fast to the tiller.

Does any aristocrat dare call that man a *day laborer?* — that man, who could trust his wife and children to God, and yield his own life, and stand at his post until his eyes were burned from their sockets, until the tiller burned under his hands, and whose last act, before his last breath, was to see if the boat was headed hard to the shore, and who would not allow himself the luxury of a death struggle, lest the course be changed. "Noble," do you say? Ah! that is a tame word.

And yet, that is but an illustration of what is hourly taking place on this earth; the divine deeds of humanity, unseen by any eye save God's, crowd a pageless catalogue; God notes them, though, every one. We think we hear God saying to that pilot, "*King John.*" Perhaps from fixed habit, and in the confusion of his first moments in the other world, John may have replied, "Ay, ay, sir!" God does not mind the reply, but announces, loud enough for all to hear, "Thou hast been faithful over a few things, I will make thee ruler over many." The real helm which that pilot held in his hands during that perilous hour, was not the helm of that boat; the real helm was an invisible one — the helm of royal state, of divine and eternal empire. *Emperor!* was that rough-faced but divine-hearted man of the sea.

See, also, that grimy but smiling engineer, whose quick eye has discovered a child, unconscious of danger, approaching the track: the speed of the locomotive is at its utmost; the distances are well measured; there is but one possibility. The noble man reverses his locomotive, then quickly glides along its side to a position of great danger, reaches out a strong arm, and catches the child when there are but twelve inches between it and death; and when the train comes to a stand-still, he kisses the *cheek* of the child, thinking the rosy lips too sweet and pure for his rough touch (they are not), sets it on its feet again, face homeward, and whistles "off brakes."

Three persons, a mother and her child, and a rough sailor heavily clad in pilot suit, were found clinging to a floating settee after shipwreck. It would support two, until the life-boat came to the rescue, but not three. The sailor looked, struggled with the conflicting thoughts of life and death for a moment, then pushed off, threw up his hands, and sank into the dark sea; the mother and child were saved.

Is there not the presence of God in such sacrifice, tenderness, and nobility? The Infinite One and such conduct are one and inseparable, and must stand or fall together. Such men are God's princes, living under mask. There is more of Christ in the common walks of life than we give credit for; indeed, there is where Christ is most apt to make his stay. Could you look through the soot upon many a man's face, you would behold — a king.

That pale-faced girl, — consumptive they called her, — who had everything to live for, but who, recalling a dreary sickness, said, "I would have nothing otherwise, for so it has pleased my Father," was one of God's queens; and they are everywhere, and often where we little expect to find them.

Are we not sometimes lifted above our former theological wonder that Christ should come to this earth and die for man? Could the universe have well overlooked it in God had he not sent his Son to redeem such fallen majesty as is wrapped up in the humblest human intelligence? Is there not good reason that God so loved the world as to give *all*, and submit to any sacrifice in its behalf? He seemed to say, Redemption for man, Redemption at any cost.

We are walking daily in the midst of a royal family, and should have a smile of good cheer, and a bow of respect, for the woman who sweeps our house, or the man who heaves our coal, or paves our streets, for they may be kings and queens *incog.*, and under masks; they may be not one step farther removed from the throne than are the most honored of us.

Three men appeared unto Abraham, but one was the Lord himself. Every man is greater than the house he lives in, and daily outgrows the garments and attainments of yesterday. "All things seem to be going about man's business, and not their own," * and no wonder. There is reason enough why the God-man walked this planet rather than any other. Emerson talks of most men as if they were "mice," and of most men and women as if only "one couple more;" he cannot be speaking of capabilities, else he knows not of what he speaks. Give a man time enough, and dispose him to application, and there is nothing within the range of possibility but he can achieve. Darwin is right in his estimate: "Man is the wonder and the glory of the *universe*."

When Chevalier Bunsen said to his wife, "In thy face have I beheld the Eternal," he spoke as Christ seems to speak of men and women. We look with solemn reverence upon the mummy, even, and justly. "It has been a temple of God: the brain has been scooped out, but the hollow once echoed with invita-

* Bacon.

tion to be just and pure." How wise the Scriptures are! Less and less do sceptics cavil their old cavils. And yet not everything has been revealed. "It doth not yet appear," "It hath not entered into the heart of man;" "thrones," "sceptres," "crowns," are — hints only. It is as if God had said, Wait, my children; I cannot tell you all at present; it is not best that you should know; but remain *true*, be not engaged with trifles, swerve not, and it shall be better than your fondest dreams.

With what startling words does revelation address men, ever urging them on to an almost restless devotion, expostulating with and imploring them.* It is as

* Illustrative are the following: "For every house is builded by some man, but he that built all things is God. And Moses verily was faithful in all his house, as a servant, for a testimony of those things which were to be spoken after: But Christ as a son over his own house: whose house are we if we hold fast the confidence and the rejoicing of the hope firm unto the end. Wherefore, as the Holy Ghost saith, To-day if ye will hear his voice, harden not your hearts, as in the provocation, in the day of temptation in the wilderness: when your fathers tempted me, proved me, and saw my works forty years. Wherefore I was grieved with that generation, and said, They do always err in their heart; and they have not known my ways. So I sware in my wrath, They shall not enter into my rest. Take heed, brethren, lest there be in any of you an evil heart of unbelief, in departing from the living God. But exhort one another daily, while it is called To-day; lest any of you be hardened through the deceitfulness of sin. For we are made partakers of Christ, if we hold the beginning of our confidence steadfast unto the end: While it is said, To-day if ye will hear his voice, harden not your hearts as in the provocation. For some, when they had heard, did provoke; howbeit, not all that came out of Egypt

if the Creator had hung placards before us with the announcement, Wanted: A race of kings! Volunteer,

by Moses. But with whom was he grieved forty years? was it not with them that had sinned, whose carcasses fell in the wilderness? And to whom sware he that they should not enter into his rest, but to them that believed not? So we see that they could not enter in because of unbelief." (Heb. iii. 4-19.)

"But thou, O man of God, flee these things: and follow after righteousness, godliness, faith, love, patience, meekness. Fight the good fight of faith, lay hold on eternal life, whereunto thou art also called, and hast professed a good profession before many witnesses. I give thee charge in the sight of God, who quickeneth all things, and before Christ Jesus, who before Pontius Pilate witnessed a good confession, that thou keep this commandment without spot, unrebukable, until the appearing of our Lord Jesus Christ: which in his times he shall show, who is the blessed and only Potentate, the King of kings, and Lord of lords; who only hath immortality, dwelling in the light which no man can approach unto, whom no man hath seen nor can see; to whom be honor and power everlasting. Amen. Charge them that are rich in this world, that they be not high-minded, nor trust in uncertain riches, but in the living God, who giveth us richly all things to enjoy; that they do good, that they be rich in good works, ready to distribute, willing to communicate; laying up in store for themselves a good foundation against the time to come, that they may lay hold on eternal life." (1 Tim. vi. 11-19.)

"Finally, my brethren, be strong in the Lord, and in the power of his might. Put on the whole armor of God, that ye may be able to stand against the wiles of the devil. For we wrestle not against flesh and blood, but against principalities, against powers, against the rulers of the darkness of this world, against spiritual wickedness in high places. Wherefore take unto you the whole armor of God, that ye may be able to withstand in the evil day, and having done all, to stand." (Eph. vi. 10-13.)

he seems to say, and the forces you need are yours. I have worlds enough for you to rule, when they are fitted up; can you count the stars? Archangels hold no positions to be envied by you. They are but God's ministers; the thrones are yours.

Immortals! you who stand amid dilapidated ruins, whose walls are riddled with the enemies' artillery, look up; above you is waving the banner of victory, bearing the sign of the cross. Issues which, without your consent, heaven itself cannot control, hang this moment pending your decision.

15

APPENDIX.

APPENDIX.

A. (Page 14.)

DR. CHALMERS, in some of the most wonderful discourses ever preached, both as regards majesty of thought and elegance of diction, has presented the affirmative of this question in the strongest possible light. They covered the preacher with a blaze of popularity, leading Mr. Wilberforce to say, that "all the world is wild about Dr. Chalmers." The following is a sample of his reasoning:—

"The world in which we live is a round ball of a determined magnitude, and occupies its own place in the firmament. But when we explore the unlimited tracts of that space which are everywhere around us, we meet with other balls of equal or superior magnitude, and from which our earth would either be invisible, or appear as small as any of those twinkling stars which are seen on the canopy of heaven.

"Why then suppose," he continues, "that this little spot—little at least in the immensity which surrounds it—should be the exclusive abode of life and of intelligence? What reason to think that those mightier globes, which roll in other parts of creation, and which we have discovered to be worlds in magnitude, are not *also* worlds in use and in dignity? Why should we think that the great Architect of nature, supreme in wisdom as he is in power, would call these stately mansions into existence, and leave them unoccupied? When we cast our eye over the broad sea, and look at the country on the other side, we see nothing but the blue land stretching obscurely over the distant horizon. We are too far away to perceive the richness of its scenery, or to hear the sound of its population. Why not extend this principle to the still more distant parts of the universe? What though, from this remote point of observation, we can see nothing but the naked roundness of yon planetary orbs? Are we, therefore, to say, that they are so many vast and unpeopled solitudes? that desolation reigns in every part of the universe but ours? that the whole energy of the divine attributes is expended on one insignificant corner of these mighty works? and that to this earth alone belongs the bloom of vegetation, or the blessedness of life, or the dignity of rational and immortal existence? . . . Who shall assign a limit to the discoveries of future ages? . . . The day may yet be coming when our instruments of observation shall be inconceivably more powerful. . . . We may see summer throwing its green mantle over these mighty tracts, and we may see them left naked and colorless after the flush of vegetation has disappeared. In the progress of years, or of centuries, we may trace the hand of cultivation spreading a new aspect over some portion of a planetary surface. Perhaps some large city, the metropolis of a mighty empire, may expand into a visible spot by the powers of some future telescope. Perhaps the glass of some observer, in a distant age, may enable him to construct a map of another world, and to lay down the surface of it in all its minute and topical varieties. But there is no end of conjecture, and to the men of other times we leave the full assurance of what we can assert with the highest probability, that yon planetary orbs are so many worlds, that they teem with life, and that the mighty Being who presides in high authority over this scene of grandeur and astonishment, has there planted worshippers of his glory."

This same line of reasoning is thus stated by Figuier: —

"What, the earth, that represents only a grain of dust lost in infinite space, shall it be the only seat of life, and shall planets a hundred times, a thousand times, fourteen hundred times larger, be only a vast grave, the one nothing in the universe, the one empty edifice in the economy of nature? Is life on our globe — that insignificant atom — to be heaped up, pressed down, and running over, filling every space, so that not a corner of its surface is empty, while in the rest of the universe not a sign of life is discoverable?"

Proctor, in "*Orbs Around Us*," presents the argument respecting Jupiter in the following form: —

"The chief arguments for the habitability of Jupiter are founded on his enormous magnitude, and the magnificence of the system which circles around him. It seems difficult to imagine that so grand an orb has been created for no special purpose, and it is equally difficult to conceive what purpose Jupiter can be said to fulfil, unless he is the abode of living creatures. He is, indeed, an object of wonder and admiration; but the mind must be singularly constituted which can accept the view that Jupiter was constructed for no other end. When every object around us suffices to exhibit the omnipotence of the Creator, we require no such evidence as is afforded by a globe exceeding the earth twelve hundred times and more in volume. The light afforded to us by Jupiter is so insignificant, also, that we cannot suppose him to have been created for no other purpose than to supply it. His influence in swaying the planetary motions is important, and he also appears to have a noteworthy influence on the sun's atmosphere; but neither influence seems necessary to the well-being of the inhabitants of earth. Thus we appear forced to concede that Jupiter has been constructed to be the abode of living creatures, unless we suppose that his function is to sway the motions of his satellites, and that these satellites are inhabited."

The great mistake in this line of argument is, that while a true absolute estimate is placed upon Jupiter, the relative grandeur of humanity is entirely overlooked. If man is what we take him to be, and if he can measure and weigh the stars and planets, that of itself is, perhaps, enough.

B. (Page 19.)

"Plurality of Worlds" states these facts in a form to render them grand and imposing: —

"The orbit of Saturn is ten times as wide as the orbit of the Earth; but beyond Saturn, and almost twice as far from the Sun, Herschel discovered Uranus, another great planet; and again, beyond Uranus, and again, at nearly twice his distance, the subtile sagacity of the astronomers of our day surmises, and then detects, another great planet. In such a system as this, the earth shrinks into insignificance. Can its concerns engage the attention of Him who made the whole? But again, the whole solar system itself, with all its orbits and planets, shrinks into a mere point, when compared with the nearest fixed star. And again, the distance which lies between us and such stars shrinks into incalculable smallness when we journey in thought to other fixed stars. And again and again, the field of our previous contemplation suffers an immeasurable contraction, as we pass on to other points of view."

General Mitchell likewise speaks of these matters with the eloquence of one who appreciates them: "As we fathom the profundity of space, and visit the island universes that stretch away in a vast illimitable perspective; when suns and systems tower in grandeur on the right hand and on the left, and the vast of space teems with glittering worlds, like sands upon the sea-shore; as we reach the nearest portion of that vast congeries of stars which we denominate the Milky Way, composed of not less than one hundred millions of suns; as we plunge yet deeper into space, and find other Milky Ways, grander and more populous in stars even than our own, until, at last, our telescopic ray extends so deeply that its length, furnishing a journey for the swift wing of more than three millions of years, fails to plunge across any other mighty depth, — then we are left to stand in a wondering and awe-struck silence upon merely the threshold of infinitude."

Yes, if we are thus left, God's purposes may have been accomplished.

C. (Page 38.)

The phenomena resulting from two suns shining upon the same planet, is well described by Figuier: —

"What strange effects must these polychromatic suns produce on the planets that they illuminate! As we know only our sun, whose light is white, it is difficult for us to imagine the odd consequences that must result from the illumination of a planetary globe and its atmosphere by the rays of blue, brown, or green suns. How queer the soil of these planets must look, the objects that stand on its surface, such as mountains and hills, and the rivers and seas, clouds and vegetation, when all are illuminated by a blue or red light, by floods of scarlet or indigo! We, who know Nature in no other guise but that which she wears on the globe in which we are confined, can hardly conceive of such effects. What, then, if we could imagine planets lighted during the same day by two successive suns of different colors! It is noon, and a blue sun inundates the globe with floods of its indigo light. The parts strongly illuminated are bright blue — a resplendent azure; those feebly illuminated are dark blue; the half tints are pale blue. Clouds, waters, and vegetation share the common hue. The stars are visible in the day-time, on account of the faint illumination of the heavens. But as the blue sun sinks, see its successor rise on the opposite horizon. It is red, and purple flashes announce its coming. One would think that a mighty conflagration lighted up the east. While on this side of the horizon the purple spreads wider and wider over the heavens, the blue rays gather about the setting sun, and color the curves of the horizon with azure reflections. What a contrast between these two illuminations, on the two sides of the heavens! and, in the interval, what strange combinations must result from the fusion of these two lights, so diverse in tone! We cannot hope to describe pictures, of which nothing around us can suggest even an approximate idea. The poet's imagination and the painter's art would be powerless to conjecture the marvellous effects that the palette of Nature realizes in these enchanted regions. Where two suns, the one red and the other green, or even one brown and the other blue, successively illuminate the same lands, what charming contrasts, what brilliant alternations, must be created by the fusion, which takes place at certain moments, of the red light and the green, or the brown light and the blue! O Nature, what wonderful aspects, what sublime perspectives, thou must put on, in those mysterious worlds, to charm the eyes of their fortunate inhabitants! And the satellites, the moons that light up the nights of their planets, what a strange spectacle must they present, in those strange realms where the eye is eternal! The moon takes on in turn the hues of the two suns, which are reflected, one after the other, on its glowing disk. The phases of the moon seen by the dwellers in these worlds are now red, now blue: hence there is a red quarter of the moon, and a blue quarter. Such a moon has a brown crescent, which succeeds a green one. When it is at the full, the moon of these parts resembles an enormous green fruit wandering in the heavens. There are moons in shades of ruby, detached on the dark ground of the firmament. Others have opaline or azure reflections. Some glitter like diamonds in their circle around the planets, which are plunged in shade. O modest moon of ours! no doubt thy peaceful light speaks to our softened and thoughtful souls; but how much deeper must be the impressions, how far more potent the charm, earnest the admiration, and intoxicating the reverence inspired in the dwellers in those far worlds, by the moons of ruby, sapphire, and emerald that illuminate the stillness and serenity of their nights!"

D. (Page 44.)

On September 7, 1871, Professor Young, of Dartmouth College, was observing a large hydrogen cloud by the sun's edge. This cloud was about one hundred thousand miles long; and its upper surface was some fifty thousand miles, the lower surface about fifteen thousand miles above the sun's surface.

The whole had the appearance of being supported on pillars of fire; these seeming pillars being in reality hydrogen jets, brighter and more active than the substance of the cloud. At half past twelve, when Professor Young chanced to be called away from his observatory, there were no indications of any approaching change, except that one of the connecting stems of the southern extremity of the cloud had grown considerably brighter, and more curiously bent to one side; and near the base of another, at the northern end, a little brilliant lump had developed itself, shaped much like a summer thunder-head.

But when Professor Young returned, about half an hour later, he found that a very remarkable change had taken place, and that a very remarkable process was actually in progress. "The whole thing had been literally blown to shreds," he says, "by some inconceivable uprush from beneath. In place of the quiet cloud I had left, the air, if I may use the expression, was filled with flying *débris*, a mass of detached vertical fusiform fragments, each from ten to thirty seconds (i. e., from four thousand five hundred to thirteen thousand five hundred miles) long by two or three seconds (nine hundred or thirteen hundred and fifty miles) wide, brighter, and closer together where the pillars had formerly stood, and rapidly ascending. When I looked, some of them had already reached a height of nearly four minutes (one hundred thousand miles); and while I watched them, they rose with a motion almost perceptible to the eye, until, in ten minutes, the uppermost were more than two hundred thousand miles above the solar surface. This was ascertained by careful measurements, the mean of three closely accordant determinations giving two hundred and ten thousand miles as the extreme altitude attained. I am particular in the statement, because, so far as I know, chromatospheric matter (red hydrogen in this case) has never before been observed at any altitude exceeding five minutes, or one hundred and thirty-five thousand miles. The velocity of ascent, also, — one hundred and sixty-seven miles per second, — is considerably greater than anything hitherto recorded. . . . As the filaments rose, they gradually faded away like a dissolving cloud, and at a quarter past one only a few filmy wisps, with some brighter streamers low down, near the chromatosphere, remained to mark the place. But in the mean while, the little "thunder-head" before alluded to had grown and developed wonderfully into a mass of rolling and ever-changing flame, to speak according to appearances. First, it was crowded down, as it were, along the solar surface; later, it rose almost pyramidally fifty thousand miles in height; then its summit was drawn down into long filaments and threads, which were most curiously rolled backwards and forwards like the volutes of an Ionic capital; and finally faded away, and by half past two had vanished, like the other. The whole phenomenon suggested most forcibly the idea of an explosion under the great prominence, acting mainly upwards, but also in all directions outwards, and then, after an interval, followed by a corresponding inrush; and it seems far from impossible that the mysterious coronal streamers, if they turn out to be truly solar, as now seems likely, may find their origin and explanation in such events."

We are indebted to Professor Winlock, of Harvard University, for the accompanying views of solar eruptions and flames. His means of taking and photographing such views are unsurpassed by any elsewhere in the world.

It is with great pleasure, also, that we confess our obligation to him for many valuable suggestions as to the data presented in the division of the book entitled "The Field."

It is due to the professor to say, also, that for the scientific errors he will not be held responsible, and that had we followed his opinions more closely, we should have been less venturesome: especially should we have placed less stress upon the irregularity of motion among the fixed stars, since the orbits of at least two (as we have since learned) seem to most astronomers to be pretty well established; but, on the other hand, we should have been far more emphatic respecting the planet Mars, for some of the statements of Mr. Proctor as to the climatology and inhabitability of that planet are treated by Professor Winlock as positively ridiculous.

E. (Page 44.)

PROFESSOR KIRCHHOFF, in his chapter on the "Physical Constitution of the Sun," says, "The most probable supposition which can be made respecting the sun's constitution is, that it consists of a solid or liquid nucleus, heated to a temperature of the brightest whiteness, surrounded by an atmosphere of somewhat lower temperature. This supposition is in accordance with La Place's celebrated nebular theory respecting the formation of our planetary system. If the matter now concentrated in the several heavenly bodies existed in former times as an extended and continuous mass of vapor, by the contraction of which, sun, planets, and moons have been formed, all these bodies must necessarily possess mainly the same constitution. Geology teaches us that the earth once existed in a state of fusion; and we are compelled to admit that the same state of things has occurred in the other members of our solar system. The amount of cooling which the various heavenly bodies have undergone, in accordance with the laws of radiation of heat, differs greatly, owing mainly to the difference in their masses. Thus, whilst the moon has become cooler than the earth, the temperature of the surface of the sun has not yet sunk below a white heat. Our terrestrial atmosphere, in which now so few elements are found, must have possessed, when the earth was in a state of fusion, a much more complicated composition, as it then contained all those substances which are volatile at a white heat. The solar atmosphere, at this time, possesses a similar constitution."

The following views are taken from the address of Sir William Thomson, at the Edinburgh meeting of the British Scientific Association, 1871: —

"The old nebular hypothesis supposes the solar system, and other similar systems through the universe, which we see at a distance as stars, to have originated in the condensation of fiery nebulous matter. This hypothesis was invented before the discovery of thermo-dynamics, or the nebulæ would not have been supposed to be fiery; and the idea seems never to have occurred to any of its inventors or early supporters, that the matter, the condensation of which they supposed to constitute the sun and stars, could have been other than fiery in the beginning. Mayer first suggested that the heat of the sun may be due to gravitation; but he supposed meteors falling in to keep always generating the heat, which is radiated, year by year, from the sun. Helmholtz, on the other hand, adopting the nebular hypothesis, showed, in 1854, that it was not necessary to suppose the nebulous matter to have been originally fiery, but that mutual gravitation between its parts may have generated the heat to which the present high temperature of the sun is due. Further, he made the important observations that the potential energy of gravitation in the sun is even now far from exhausted; but that, with further and further shrinking, more and more heat is to be generated, and that thus we can conceive the sun now to possess a sufficient store of energy to produce heat and light, almost as at present, for several million years of time future. It ought, however, to be added, that this condensation can only follow from cooling, and therefore that Helmholtz's gravitational explanation of future sun-heat amounts really to showing that the sun's thermal capacity is enormously greater, in virtue of the mutual gravitation between the parts of so enormous a mass, than the sum of the thermal capacities of separate and smaller bodies, of the same material and same total mass.

"For a few years, Mayer's theory of solar heat had seemed to me probable; but I had been led to regard it as no longer tenable, because I had been in the first place driven, by consideration of the very approximate constancy of the earth's period of revolution round the sun for the last two thousand years, to conclude that 'the principal source, perhaps the sole appreciably effective source, of sun heat is in bodies circulating round the sun at present inside the earth's orbit;' and because Leverrier's researches on the motion of the planet Mercury, though giving evidence of a sensible influence attributable to matter circulating as a great number of small planets within his orbit round the sun, showed that the amount of matter that could possibly be assumed to circulate at any considerable distance from the sun must be very small; and therefore, 'if the meteoric influx taking place at present is enough to produce any appreciable portion of the heat radiated away, it must be supposed to be from matter circulating round the sun, within very short distances of his surface. The density of this meteoric cloud would have to be supposed so great, that comets could scarcely have escaped as comets actually have escaped, showing no discoverable effects of resistance, after passing his surface within a distance equal to one eighth of his radius. All things considered, there seems little probability in the hypothesis that solar radiation is compensated, to any appreciable degree, by heat generated by meteors falling in at present; and as it can be shown that no chemical theory is tenable, it must be concluded as most probable that the sun is at present merely an incandescent liquid mass cooling.'

"Thus, on purely astronomical grounds, was I long ago led to abandon as very improbable the hypothesis that the sun's heat is supplied dynamically, from year to year, by the influx of meteors. But now, spectrum analysis gives proof finally conclusive against it."

It is Professor Winlock's opinion that the sun is neither solid nor liquid, but gaseous throughout.

F. (Page 46.)

The following is the method by which Wolf is facetiously represented as reaching his conclusions:—

"It is shown, in optics, that the pupil of the eye dilates and contracts, according to the degree of light it encounters. Wherefore, since in Jupiter the sun's meridian height is much weaker than on the earth, the pupil will need to be much more dilatable in the Jovial creature than in the terrestrial one. But the pupil is observed to have a constant proportion to the ball of the eye, and the ball of the eye to the rest of the body; so that, in animals, the larger the pupil, the larger the eye, and consequently the larger the body. Assuming that these conditions are unquestionable, he shows that Jupiter's distance from the sun, compared with the earth's, is as twenty-six to five. The intensity of the sun's light in Jupiter is to its intensity on the earth, in a duplicate ratio, five to twenty-six. The eyes of the Jovians, and their dimensions generally, must be correspondingly enlarged, and it therefore follows that even Goliath of Gath would have cut but a sorry figure among the natives of Jupiter. That is, supposing the Philistine's altitude to be somewhere between eight feet and eleven, according as we lean to Bishop Cumberland's calculation, or the Vatican copy of the Septuagint. Now, Wolfius proves the size of the inhabitants of Jupiter to be the same as that of Og, king of Bashan, whose iron camp-bed was nine cubits in length, and four in breadth; or rather he shows, in the way stated, the ordinary altitude of the Jovicolæ to be $13\frac{819}{1440}$ Paris feet, and the height of Og to have been $13\frac{1296}{1440}$ feet."

Proctor shows, in the following manner, how easily an entirely different conclusion may be reached: —

"We, on the other hand," he says, "are led to the conclusion that the Jovicolæ are pygmies, about two and a half feet, on an average, in height. For we know that a man, removed to Jupiter, would weigh about two and a half times as much as he does on our own earth. He would thus be oppressed with a burden equivalent to half as much again as his own weight. This would render life itself an insupportable burden: and we have to inquire what difference of size would suffice to make a Joveman as active as our terrestrial man. Now, the weight of bodies similarly proportioned varies as the third power of the height. For example, a body twice as high as another in other respects similar, will be eight times as heavy. But the muscular power of animals varies as the cross section of corresponding muscles, or obviously as the square of the linear dimensions; so that, of two animals similarly constituted, but one twice as high as the other, the larger would be four times the more powerful. He would weigh, however, eight times as much as the other. He would therefore be only half as active. Similarly, an animal three times as high as another of similar build, would be only one third as active; and so on for all such relations. Now, since a terrestrial man, removed to Jupiter, would be two and a half times as heavy as on the earth, it follows, obviously, that a man on Jupiter, proportioned like our terrestrial men, would be as active as they are, if his height were to theirs as one to two and a half. Hence, setting six feet as the maximum ordinary height of men on earth, we see that the tallest and handsomest of the Jovicolæ can be but two and a half feet in height, *if only our premises are correct.* Thus Tom Thumb, and other little fellows, if removed to Jupiter, might be wondered at for their enormous height, and eagerly sought after by any Carlylian Fredericks who may be forming grenadier corps out yonder."

Other views have also been advanced, which we have no space to insert in full, snch as that the inhabitants of Jupiter are bat-winged; are inveterate dancers; that the bodies of the Jovials are composed of numerous convolutions of tubes, more analogous to the trunk of the elephant than anything else;* that they are pulpy, gelatinous creatures, living in a dismal world of water and ice, with a cindery nucleus; † that they may have their homes in subterranean cities warmed by central fires, or in crystal caves cooled by ocean tides, or may float with Nereids upon the deep, or mount upon wings as eagles. ‡

It is amusing, in other respects, to note the diverse conclusions reached by different writers. Emmanuel Kant, for instance, advances the theory that souls, in their imperfect state, start from the sun, travelling outward from planet to planet, and reaching paradise at length in the most remote and coldest planet of all.

The astronomer Bode, on the other hand, represents that we start in our transmigratory journey from the remotest planets, advancing progressively from one planet to another towards the sun, which is the astronomical paradise and abode of the most perfect beings in creation. For which views, see M. Flammarion's "Les Modes Imaginaires."

* Sir Humphry Davy. † Whewell. ‡ Brewster.

There is another matter which Charles Bonnet, Dupont of Nemours, Jean Reynaud, Bode, Kant, and Figuier have introduced into the subject, which seems to us much out of place. It assumes this form: Though the astronomical bodies are uninhabitable by human agents, they are not by spiritual agents. They are therefore the abodes of our departed friends, and the homes of angels.

It is our privilege here, as before, to conjecture anything we please. But, to be reasonable, we are compelled to say that the souls of the dead, and angelic existences, are not physical; consequently the condition of the planets and the stars, inhabited or uninhabited, can make no difference with angels and the spirits of the departed. Their homes, we can rest assured, are not upon any physical and material object in space. It is rather in the invisible and spiritual heavens, where there are "many mansions." Elsewhere than in the starry heavens will unfold to the true children of God many vacant areas, upon which they can pitch their sacred and substantial pavilions. Though invisible to a physical eye, God will provide — has provided. The physical universe is for other purposes, not for this.

G. (Page 88.)

Among those who have tried to mitigate the circumstances attending the crime of Judas, W. W. Story has not been surpassed, perhaps, especially in point of interest and ingenuity. The title, "A Roman Lawyer in Jerusalem," is suggestive of his method of treatment. The following extracts will be of interest. First, the question at issue is stated: —

> "The question is, Did Judas, doing this,
> Act from base motives, and commit a crime?
> Or, all things taken carefully in view,
> Can he be justified in what he did?"

Judas is then compared with the other disciples: —

"Those who went with him and believed in him
Were mostly dull, uneducated men,
Simple and honest, dazed by what he did,
And misconceiving every word he said.
He led them with him in a spell-bound awe,
And all his cures they called miraculous.

"'What! all — all fled?' I asked. 'Did none remain?'

"'Not one,' he said; 'all left him to his fate.
Not one dared own he was a follower;
Not one gave witness for him of them all.
Stop! When I say not one of them, I mean
No one but Judas, — Judas, whom they call
The traitor, — who betrayed him to his death.
He rushed into the council-hall, and cried,
"'Tis I have sinned — Christus is innocent."'

"'The truth is truth, and let the truth be told.
Judas, I say, alone of all the men
Who followed Christus, thought that he was God.
Some feared him for his power of miracles;
Some were attracted by a sort of spell;
Some followed him to hear his sweet, clear voice,
And gentle speaking, hearing with their ears,
And knowing not the sense of what he said;
But one alone believed he was the Lord,
The true Messiah of the Jews. That one
Was Judas, — he alone of all the crowd.'

"'He to betray his Master for a bribe!
He last of all! I say this friend of mine
Was brave when all the rest were cowards there.'

"'His was a noble nature: frank and bold,
Almost to rashness bold, yet sensitive,
Who took his dreams for firm realities;
Who once believing, all in all believed;

Rushing at obstacles and scorning risk,
Ready to venture all to gain his end;
No compromise or subterfuge for him,
His act went from his thought straight to the butt;
Yet with this ardent and impatient mood
Was joined a visionary mind, that took
Impressions quick and fine, yet deep as life.
Therefore it was that in this subtile soil
The Master's words took root, and grew, and flowered.
He heard, and followed, and obeyed; his faith
Was serious, earnest, real — winged to fly;
He doubted not, like some who walked with him;
Desired no first place, as did James and John;
Denied him not with Peter: not to him
His Master said, "Away! thou'rt an offence;
Get thee behind me, Satan!" — not to him,
"Am I so long with ye who know me not?"
Fixed as a rock, untempted by desires
To gain the post of honor when his Lord
Should come to rule — chosen from out the midst
Of six-score men as his apostle — then
Again selected to the place of trust,
Unselfish, honest, he among them walked.

"'That he was honest, and was so esteemed,
Is plain from this, — they chose him out of all
To bear the common purse, and take, and pay.
John says he was a thief, because he grudged
The price that for some ointment once was paid,
And urged 'twere better given to the poor.
But did not Christus ever for the poor
Lift up his voice, — "Give all things to the poor;
Sell everything and give all to the poor!"
And Judas, who believed, not made believe,
Used his own words, and Christus, who excused
The gift because of love, rebuked him not.
Thief! ay, he 'twas, this very thief, they chose
To bear the purse, and give alms to the poor.
I, for my part, see nothing wrong in this.'

"'But why, if Judas was a man like this,
Frank, noble, honest,'—here I interposed,—
'Why was it that he thus betrayed his Lord?'

"'This question oft did I revolve,' said he,
'When all the facts were fresh, and oft revolved
In later days, and with no change of mind;
And this is my solution of the case:—

"'Daily he heard his Master's voice proclaim,
"I am the Lord! the Father lives in me!
Who knoweth me knows the Eternal God!
He who believes in me shall never die!
No! he shall see me with my angels come
With power and glory here upon the earth
To judge the quick and dead! Among you here
Some shall not taste of death before I come
God's kingdom to establish on the earth!"

"'What meant these words? They seethed in Judas' soul.
"Here is my God—Messias, King of kings,
Christus, the Lord—the Saviour of us all.
How long shall he be taunted and reviled,
And threatened by this crawling scum of men?
O, who shall urge the coming of that day
When he in majesty shall clothe himself,
And stand before the astounded world its King?"
Long brooding over this inflamed his soul;
And, ever rash in schemes as wild in thought,
At last he said, "No longer will I bear
This ignominy heaped upon my Lord.
No man hath power to harm the Almighty One.
Ay, let men's hand be lifted, then, at once,
Effulgent like the sun, swift like the sword,
The jagged lightning-flashes from the cloud,
Shall he be manifest—the living God—
And prostrate all shall on the earth adore!"'"

The following extract from De Quincey will sufficiently express his effort to exonerate Judas: —

"Everything connected with our ordinary conceptions of this man, Judas Iscariot, of his real purposes, and of his scriptural doom, apparently is erroneous. Not one thing, but all things, must rank as false which traditionally we accept about him. That neither any motive of his, nor any ruling impulse, was tainted with the vulgar treachery imputed to him, appears probable from the strength of his remorse. And this view of his case comes recommended by so much of internal plausibility, that in Germany it has long since shaped itself into the following distinct hypothesis: Judas Iscariot, it is alleged, participated in the common delusion of the apostles as to that earthly kingdom which, under the sanction and auspices of Christ, they supposed to be waiting and ripening for the Jewish people. So far there was nothing in Judas to warrant any special wonder or any separate blame. If *he* erred, so did the other apostles. But in one point Judas went farther than his brethren — viz., in speculating upon the *reasons* of Christ for delaying the inauguration of this kingdom. All things were apparently ripe for it; all things pointed to it; the expectation and languishing desires of many Hebrew saints — viz., the warning from signs; the prophetic alarms propagated by heralds like the Baptist; the mysterious interchange of kindling signals rising suddenly out of darkness as secret words between distant parties — secret question or secret answer; the fermentation of revolutionary doctrines all over Judea; the passionate impatience of the Roman yoke; the continual openings of new convulsions at the great centre of Rome; the insurrectionary temper of Jewish society, as indicated by the continual rise of robber leaders, that drew off multitudes into the neighboring deserts; and, universally, the unsettled mind of the Jewish nation, their deep unrest, and the anarchy of their expectations. These explosive materials had long been accumulated; they needed only a kindling spark. Heavenly citations to war, divine summonses to resistance, had long been read in the insults and aggressions of paganism; there wanted only a leader. And such a leader, if he would but consent to assume that office, stood ready in the founder of Christianity. The supreme qualifications for leadership, manifested and emblazoned in the person of Jesus Christ, were evident to *all* parties in the Jewish community, and not merely to the religious body of his own immediate followers. These qualifications were published and expounded to the world in the facility with which everywhere he drew crowds about himself, in the extraordinary depth of impression which attended his teaching, and in the fear, as well as hatred, which possessed the Jewish rulers against him. Indeed, so great was this fear, so great was this hatred, that, had it not been for the predominance of the Roman element in the government of Judea, it is pretty certain that Christ would have been crushed in an earlier stage of his career.

"Believing, therefore, as Judas did, and perhaps had reason to do, that Christ contemplated the establishment of a temporal kingdom — the restoration, in fact, of David's throne; believing also that all the conditions towards the realization of such a scheme met and centred in the person of Christ, what was it that, upon any solution intelligible to Judas, neutralized so grand a scheme of promise? Simply and obviously, to a man with the views of Judas, it was the character of Christ himself, sublimely over-gifted for purposes of speculation, but, like Shakespeare's great creation of Prince Hamlet, not correspondingly endowed for the business of action, and the clamorous emergencies of life. Indecision and doubt (such was the interpretation of Judas) crept over the faculties of the Divine Man as often as he was summoned away from his own natural Sabbath of heavenly contemplation to the gross necessities of action. It became important, therefore, according to the views adopted by Judas, that his Master should be *precipitated* into action by a force from without, and thrown into the centre of some popular movement, such as, once beginning to revolve, could not afterwards be suspended or checked. Christ must be *compro-*

mised before doubts could have time to form. It is by no means improbable that this may have been the theory of Judas. Nor is it at all necessary to seek for the justification of such a theory, considered as a matter of prudential policy, in Jewish fanaticism. The Jews of that day were distracted by internal schisms. Else, and with any benefit from national unity, the headlong rapture of Jewish zeal, when combined in vindication of their insulted temple and temple-worship, would have been equal to the effort of dislodging the Roman legionary force, *for the moment*, from the military possession of Palestine. After which, although the restoration of the Roman supremacy could not ultimately have been evaded, it is by no means certain that a *temperamentum*, or reciprocal scheme of concessions, might not have been welcome at Rome, such as had, in fact, existed under Herod the Great and his father. The radical power, under such a scheme, would have been lodged in Rome, but with such external concessions to Jewish nationality as might have consulted the real interests of both parties. Administered under Jewish names, the land would have yielded a larger revenue than, as a refractory nest of insurgents, it ever *did* yield to the Roman exchequer; and, on the other hand, a ferocious bigotry, which was really sublime in its indomitable obstinacy, might have been humored without prejudice to the grandeur of the *imperial* claims. Even little Palmyra, in later times, was indulged to a greater extent, without serious injury in any quarter, had it not been for the feminine arrogance in little insolent Zenobia, that misinterpreted and abused that indulgence.

"The miscalculation, in fact, of Judas Iscariot — supposing him really to have entertained the views ascribed to him — did not hinge at all upon political oversights, but upon a total spiritual blindness; in which blindness, however, he went no farther than at that time did probably most of his brethren. Upon *them*, quite as little as upon *him*, had yet dawned the true grandeur of the Christian scheme. In this only he outran his brethren — that, sharing, in their blindness, he greatly exceeded them in presumption. All alike

had imputed to their Master views utterly irreconcilable with the grandeur of his new and heavenly religion. It was no religion at all which they, previously to the crucifixion, supposed to be the object of Christ's teaching; it was a mere preparation for a pitiably vulgar scheme of earthly aggrandizement. But, whilst the other apostles had simply failed to comprehend their Master, Judas had presumptuously assumed that he *did* comprehend him, and understood his purposes better than Christ himself. His object was audacious in a high degree, but (according to the theory which I am explaining) for that very reason not treacherous at all. The more that he was liable to the approach of audacity, the less can he be suspected of perfidy. He supposed himself executing the very innermost purposes of Christ, but with an energy which it was the characteristic infirmity of Christ to want. He fancied that by *his* vigor of action were fulfilled those great political changes which Christ approved, but wanted audacity to realize. His hope was, that, when at length actually arrested by the Jewish authorities, Christ would no longer vacillate; he would be forced into giving the signal to the populace of Jerusalem, who would then rise unanimously, for the double purpose of placing Christ at the head of an insurrectionary movement and of throwing off the Roman yoke. As regards the worldly prospects of this scheme, it is by no means improbable that Iscariot was right. It seems, indeed, altogether impossible that he, who (as the treasurer of the apostolic fraternity) had in all likelihood the most of worldly wisdom, and was best acquainted with the temper of the times, could have made any gross blunder as to the wishes and secret designs of the populace in Jerusalem."

John Henry Newman and Archbishop Whately present nothing essentially different in their treatment of the case. The chief trouble with all these views is a vital one, namely, they are not in harmony with scriptural representation. It is about equally easy to explain away the deviltry of the devil, as thus to excuse the treachery of Judas.

H. (Page 110.)

The description given of the murder, by Mr. Webster, in the trial of the Knapps, applies to every guilty person when conscience is aroused: —

"He has done the murder. No eye has seen him. No ear has heard him. The secret is his own, and it is safe. Ah, gentlemen, that was a dreadful mistake. Such a secret can be safe nowhere. The whole creation of God has neither nook nor corner where the guilty can bestow it, and say it is safe. Not to speak of that eye which pierces through all disguises, and beholds everything as in the splendor of noon, such secrets of guilt are never safe from detection, even by men. True it is, generally speaking, that "murder will out." True it is that Providence hath so ordained, and doth so govern things, that those who break the great law of Heaven, by shedding man's blood, seldom succeed in avoiding discovery. Especially in a case exciting so much attention as this, discovery must come, and will come, sooner or later. A thousand eyes turn at once to explore every man, every thing, every circumstance connected with the time and place. A thousand ears catch every whisper. A thousand excited minds intensely dwell on the scene, shedding all their light, and ready to kindle the slightest circumstance into a blaze of discovery. Meantime the guilty soul cannot keep its own secret. It is false to itself; or, rather, it feels an irresistible impulse of conscience to be true to itself. It labors under its guilty possession, and knows not what to do with it. The human heart was not made for the residence of such an inhabitant. It finds itself preyed on by a torment which it dares not acknowledge to God or man. A vulture is devouring it, and it can ask no sympathy or assistance, either from heaven or earth. The secret which the murderer possesses soon comes to possess him; and, like the evil spirit of which we read, it overcomes him, and leads him withersoever it will. He feels it beating at his heart, rising to his throat, and demanding disclosure, He thinks the whole world sees it in his face, reads it in his eyes, and almost hears its workings in the very silence of his thoughts. It has become his master. It betrays his discretion, it breaks down his courage, it conquers his prudence. When suspicion from without begin to embarrass him, and the net of circumstance to entangle him, the fatal secret struggles with still greater violence to burst forth. It must be confessed, it will be confessed; there is no refuge from confession but suicide, and suicide is confession."

Shakespeare depicts no less vividly the working of a guilty conscience: —

> "O coward conscience, how dost thou afflict me! —
> The lights burn blue. — It is now dead midnight.
> Cold, fearful drops stand on my trembling flesh.
> What do I fear? Myself? There's none else by!
> Richard loves Richard; that is, I am I.
> Is there a murderer here? No: — yes; I am.
> Then fly. What, from myself? Great reason; why?
> Lest I revenge. What! myself upon myself?
> I love myself. Wherefore? for any good
> That I myself have done unto myself?
> O, no: alas! I rather hate myself
> For hateful deeds committed by myself.
> I am a villain: yet I lie; I am not.
> Fool, of thyself speak well. Fool, do not flatter.
> My conscience hath a thousand several tongues,
> And every tongue brings in a several tale,
> And every tale condemns me for a villain.
> Perjury, perjury, in the high'st degree;
> Murder, stern murder, in the dir'st degree;
> All several sins, all used in each degree,
> Throng to the bar, crying all — Guilty! guilty!
> I shall despair. — There is no creature loves me;
> And if I die, no soul will pity me: —
> Nay, wherefore should they? since that I myself
> Find in myself no pity for myself.
> Methought the souls of all that I had murdered
> Came to my tent; and every one did threat
> To-morrow's vengeance on the head of Richard."

I. (Page 120.)

Wemyss states some things respecting the Book of Job so fairly that we cannot well forbear direct quotation :—

"DESIGN OF THE BOOK.

"That temporal calamities are not always sent as punishments of sin, but simply as trials of faith and patience, and as instructive examples to others. That submission to the will of Heaven is not only the indispensable duty of afflicted persons, but the most probable means of procuring their deliverance and restoration. That God doth not willingly afflict the children of men, but has always some higher purpose in view, — that his administration of the world must be an equitable one, since it could be no profit to him to oppress his creatures, — that God deals with every being in his immense family in a manner suited to its nature, wants, and destination, — that in his sight nothing is too lofty, nothing too low; that the hawk flies by his wisdom, and the eagle soars at his command; that even the frightful crocodile and the huge rhinoceros are the objects of his care, and masterpieces of divine workmanship. That pain, disease, poverty, bereavement, in every case, have some higher end than the mere arbitrary infliction of calamity, — that the sum and substance of human comfort, in times of trial, is a humble but firm confidence in God, — that the divine eye is always open and attentive to the affairs and actions of his human offspring, and that there is a close connection between the divine superintendence and the subordinate causes and effects that arise in the natural and moral world. That God needs not the vindication of his character by his creatures, but can always undertake his own defence; that as the prosperity of the wicked is not of long duration, so neither is the calamity of the righteous; that the wicked are sometimes exalted, only to make their fall more conspicuous; that the righteous are sometimes depressed and apparently deserted only to make the divine regard for them more eminently and triumphantly seen. Such are some of the principal maxims which it appears to be the design of the book to inculcate. The whole seems intended to demonstrate the insufficiency of human reason, and the rashness of men, whether in attempting to fathom the depths of divine Providence in the government of the universe, or in pronouncing dogmatically on the causes of the happiness or misery of individual men.

"All this is effected, not in a dry, formal, didactic way, but by means of an animated and prolonged discussion, each speaker taking his turn, and all being seated, according to the manner of the East. The whole is carried on in a style highly figurative and poetical, and embellished with a profusion of splendid images. Each speaker, as is common in such discussions, is represented as retaining his own opinions. An interlocutor appears, and places the subject in a different light. He is interrupted by the appearance of the Deity. A thunder-storm is formed in the distance, and draws nearer. A profound silence reigns throughout nature; at length an awful peal is heard; the cloud bursts, and there proceeds from it a majestic voice, which, in a series of unanswerable interrogations, makes manifest that his power is irresistible and his counsels inscrutable; that the first and best duty of his creatures is unreserved submission to his will, and an entire confidence in his decisions. The whole is calculated to produce the deepest humility in man, and to lead to the most exalted conceptions of God.

"Thus the book is a continual and enduring lesson on the providence of the Creator and our dependence, — on his power and our weakness, — on his greatness and our nothingness.

"Besides all this, the book has singular attractions, on account of its prodigious antiquity, being by far the oldest of all the books that have come down to our times, and including fragments of didactic poetry which probably belonged to the antediluvian period. It is also a kind of patriarchal encyclopædia, as containing distinct, though brief, traces of philosophy, morals, and history, as existing in these remote ages. The reader is transported into a distant land, in times not far removed from the cradle of the human race; he finds himself in a new region, amongst men and manners previously unknown. Everything wears a primitive, simple, and foreign aspect. The countenance of the people is grave, their manner dignified, their speech oracular. The fire and eagerness of the Eastern character are ready to burst forth, but the calmness and philosophy of the sage repress them. Their religious views are simple, but sublime: they know God, and revere him; and each, in his own way, is indignant at any attack made on the equity of the Supreme Governor; but they know nothing of the immortality of the soul, or of a world to come. Neither do they seem to have had any glimpse of a Redeemer, unless it were through the medium of the one rite of sacrifice, of which they would probably inquire the meaning, or they might learn traditionally the early promise of the victory to be obtained, at some future period, over the serpent, by the woman's seed. Of all this, however, there is no trace in the book.

"To those who have suffered affliction, and whose tranquillity has been repeatedly broken by painful visitations, this book affords inestimable resources in the way of consolation; and to those who are of a contemplative and serious mind, there is no work more fit to make us feel the inanity of all human things, to detach our hearts from present scenes, and to direct our thoughts towards a better world."

"IT IS NOT A DRAMATIC COMPOSITION.

"The book has been supposed by some to possess a dramatic character; but this opinion is contradicted by the style of the commencement and close, which are undoubtedly narrative; also by the regular intervention of the historian himself at the beginning of every speech, to inform us of the name of the speaker. Besides, there is no *action* in the work, and action is essential to the drama: all is still and quiet, and exhibits merely the tenor of ordinary colloquy. Long discourses of an argumentative kind, and proverbial sentences, constitute the essence of the book. There is a certain kind of division and arrangement in the conferences, but there are no *scenes*, in the dramatic sense of that term. We have a meeting of eastern sages, who dispute about the order of Providence, as exemplified in the patriarch's case; a sort of contest on the real cause of God's visitation of Job; consequently there is no drama.

"Neither is it necessary to characterize the composition farther than by saying that, except its exordium and its close, it is undoubtedly poetical from beginning to end: and some persons, such as Jerome, go so far as to say, that it is written in hexameter verses, consisting of dactyls and spondees; but this is an assertion difficult to verify, as we have long since lost the true pronunciation of the Hebrew language. Jerome himself acknowledges that other feet frequently occur, and that the measure of the verses often differs in the number of the syllables of the several feet. We consider the whole of this as matter of conjecture.

"As to the form of its composition, consisting of several discourses, delivered by different interlocutors, and which appear too refined and sublime for mere extemporary effusions, the Orientals were well known to have been fond of such meetings, and of holding long conversations and reasonings, in elevated expressions and proverbial phrases, proposed and answered with an eloquent facility. We are not bound to suppose that these conferences were held at one sitting, but took place according to the feelings and convenience of the several speakers. It is not at all probable that the whole happened without interruption, rest. or refreshment. If the friends, during the first interview, remained seven days and seven nights, without speaking a word, the subsequent discourses must have taken place after certain intervals. Of these discourses there are nine series, each of which must have occupied at least one day. in the slow, deliberate, and sententious manner of Eastern conversation and discussion, which has more of the solemn and oracular form than is consistent with our modern flippancy and fluency. Nor would it be surprising if the space of one day at least intervened between these different conferences, or even more than that;

and it is scarcely to be thought that Job's disease would allow him to carry on such frequent colloquies, without intermissions of repose. However this may be, there is a perfect unity of design in the whole composition; and whether viewed in the light of a merely literary production, an inspired narrative, or a faithful record of actual facts, it carries with it all the marks of a very remote antiquity.

"Still there are some parts of the book which have much of a dramatic character. The three friends recite their parts. Job replies to each of them in turn. Nothing is decided or brought to issue. At length a spectator interferes, and courteously begs leave to take a part, after the others had exhausted their materials of disputation. He speaks well, but not with sufficient authority to close the controversy. At last the Almighty interposes, pronounces sentence on all parties, and awards each his due. This is the *finale*, or winding up of the scene. It is to be inferred, too, from several passages, that an audience was present at the whole debate, who, no doubt, took a lively interest in the scene, their sympathies being roused or repressed according to the convictions produced in their minds by the different speakers in their turn.

"But though all this be true, still, to call the poem a drama, or a tragedy, or the like, would be highly absurd, since that species of composition was utterly unknown in Job's day, and was a modern invention of the Greeks, who lived near the 100th Olympiad; that is to say, which was not known till about four centuries before the birth of Jesus Christ. Epigenes or Thespis being the first inventors of Tragedy, and Eupolis or Cratinus those of Comedy, more than two thousand years after the computed time of Job.

"Were the book a mere dramatic composition, the work of some unknown poet, it would not have been written as it is; for Poetry, like Painting, endeavors to conceal the defects of its subject, by throwing some drapery over them; whereas, here we have not only represented to us Job's patience, but his impatience, — not merely his resignation, but his murmurs, — not simply his faith, but his despair. He feels everything with deep sensibility; he passes rapidly from one passion to its contrary; he is now irritated, then calmed; now he implores pity, then he demands justice; he now addresses God as a tender father, then he complains of him as a severe master; he loves life, and yet he sighs for death; he smiles on meeting with a sepulchre, he shudders on the brink of a tomb. His weaknesses are brought out fully on the canvas; and this is the supreme beauty of Holy Writ, in all its parts, that there is no attempt made to *conceal* human deformity, any more than to exaggerate it; the only anxiety of Scripture being to do justice to the *Divine* character, to represent the great Parent in endearing aspects, and to vindicate the ways of God to man."

"JOB A REAL PERSON.

"Whether such a personage as Job ever existed has been made a matter of dispute by some; but the affirmative side of the question appears plain, when we find him ranked by Ezekiel with Noah and Daniel (chap. xiv. 14, 20), and referred to, in the most explicit manner, by James (chap. v. 11), who, wishing to recommend patience by an example, referred his countrymen to this book.

"Besides this, his country and his circumstances being so particularly described, together with the names of his friends, and those of his family, we cannot help concluding that it is to be considered as a real history. Their discourses, too, are distinctly set down, and are specially directed to the condition in which he was placed.

"Nor would the example of a *fictitious* character carry with it half the weight in inculcating the virtue of patience, or any other virtue, as that of a real sufferer, distinguished by the magnanimous feeling and elevated understanding which are here attributed to Job. Viewing him as a person who once actually existed, this book is exactly the memorial which he himself wished for; a memorial more permanent than any that could be engraved in brass, or carved on a rock. The memorial is interwoven with the sacred canon, and has been, and will be, handed down to all generations who are made acquainted with the law of God.

"If the silence of other sacred writers respecting Job be remarked, let it first be inquired, whether they knew anything of his history, and whether they were under any obligation to mention it.

"The history of Job is too circumstantial to be a mere fiction. Not only is his name given, and the place of his abode, but his dispositions, his integrity, his faith, his patience, his dignity, his fortitude, are all distinctly exemplified. Even his failings are enumerated, and his murmurs as carefully recorded as his thanksgivings. We have also the names and lineage of his friends, the numbers of his children, the names of his latest daughters, the age which he arrived at, — all of them bearing marks of a real and veritable history rather than of a fictitious narrative. Arabian writers, too, and the Koran in particular, always make mention of Job as a real person, whose descendants were considered as remaining among them at a late period; and his grave is shown in the East at this day. That it is shown in six different places, just as seven cities contended for the honor of being viewed as the birthplace of Homer, does not invalidate, but confirm, the fact of his existence. The most celebrated tomb is that of the Trachonites, towards the springs of Jordan. It is situated between the cities still bearing the names of Teman, Shuah, and Naama. There is another tomb publicly shown for that of the pătriarch, in Armenia; and a third near the walls of Constantinople; which last more probably belonged to an Arabian warrior of the same name, who fell at the siege of that city, in 672."

"THE MORALITY OF JOB.

"The severe charges against his character, either directly or by marked insinuation, made by Job's professed friends, in the course of their dialogues with him, obliged the holy patriarch to enter into a vindication of himself, and to appeal to his former conduct during the season of his prosperity. From this vindication we learn what his moral principles were, and they appear less to resemble those involved in the code of laws given to Moses, than those promulgated in the Sermon on the Mount by Jesus Christ. The Decalogue says, 'Thou shalt not commit adultery;' in which form of expression we recognize a prohibition of the actual crime, but no reference to the inward sentiment. In the law of Christ, not only is the actual crime forbidden, but the unchaste desire of the mind, which is the embryo of the overt act. (Matt. v. 28.) In exact conformity to which, we find the patriarch saying, chap. xxxi. 1, —

'I made a covenant with *mine eyes*,
That I would not *gaze* upon *a virgin*.
For what portion should I then have in God,
Or what inheritance of the Almighty from on high?'

And this he grounds upon two considerations — the consequences of transgression, and the omniscience of God: —

'Doth not destruction follow the wicked,
And shame pursue the workers of iniquity? —
Doth not the Eternal see my ways,
And number all my footsteps?'

He goeth farther than this, and not merely disclaims all mental impurity which might be excited by the contemplation of virgin beauty, but denies that still baser feeling which might prompt to the destruction of another's conjugal happiness: —

'If my heart hath been enticed to a *married woman*,
Or I have lain in wait at my neighbor's door,
Then let my wife gratify another,
And let others bow down upon her;
For this is *the basest wickedness*,
And a crime to be punished by the Judge;
It is a fire consuming to destruction;
It would root out all mine increase.'

"Such are the noble sentiments of Job in regard to this part of the Divine Law — sentiments that would do honor to any era of the world, and in entire congeniality with the gospel of Christ.

"Overwhelmed by accumulated calamities as Job was, and therefore strongly tempted to abridge his own existence by violent means, we find him not merely revolting from this impious practice, but calmly professing his determination to abide the issue: —

'All the days of my appointed time
I will wait, till my release shall come.'

"This thorough confidence in God, as one who does not afflict willingly, nor grieve the children of men, is in striking contrast to the conduct of those, who, whenever their prospects are clouded, rush to self-destruction as a relief: —

'When all the blandishments of life are gone,
The sinner creeps to death — the saint lives on.'

"The examples of Achitophel and Judas are quite sufficient, were there no other reasons for deterring, to bring this dreadful crime into utter disrepute.

"The worship of the One True God, to the exclusion of all false deities, is plainly an article in the patriarch's creed. Sabaism, or the adoration of the celestial luminaries, was probably the only species of idolatry existing in Job's time; and for aught we know, had become prevalent in his and in the neighboring countries. But how indignantly does he renounce every departure of this kind from the allegiance he owed to Jehovah, when he says, —

'If I have looked with a superstitious eye
At the sun, when he shone in his strength,
Or the moon, when she walked in her brightness,
And my heart hath been secretly enticed,
And I have worshipped by carrying my hand to my mouth,
I should have been chargeable with a great transgression,
For I should have denied the Supreme God.'

"An abhorrence of deceit is also a feature in the moral

character of Job. Any attempt to *overreach* his neighbor, or even to *covet* what belonged to him, still more to *accept a bribe* as an inducement to perpetrate injustice, he pronounces to be far from his thoughts. He says, —

> 'If I have acted fraudulently,
> And my foot hath hastened to dishonesty,
> Let me be weighed in a just balance,
> That God may know mine integrity.
> If my step hath turned from the right way,
> And my heart hath gone after mine eyes;
> If any bribe hath cleaved to my hands,
> Then may I sow and another eat;
> Let another root out what I have planted.'

"A man's soundness of principle may safely be judged of by his conduct towards the members of his own family, and especially towards his domestic servants. In this point of view Job's character stands very high, since he professes before God, as well as before man, a conscientious regard to his dependants, and a determination to treat them equitably

> 'If I denied justice to my man-servant,
> Or to my maid-servant, when they disputed with me,
> What then should I do, when God maketh inquest?
> When He inquires, what answer should I give?
> Did not He who formed me form them?
> Were we not fashioned alike in the womb?'

"In ancient times, slaves had no action at law against their owners; they might dispose of them as they did of their cattle, or any other property. The slave might complain, and the owner might hear him if he pleased, but he was not compelled to do so. Job states that he had admitted his servants to all civil rights; and, far from preventing their case from being heard, he was ready to permit them to complain even against himself, if they had a cause of complaint, and to give them all the benefit of the law.

"Strict equity in dealing, though in itself laudable, is insufficient to constitute a man truly amiable in the eyes of his fellow-men, unless it be accompanied by frequent acts of benevolence and charity; proving that, though justice be the rule of his conduct, compassion and generosity dwell with it in the same bosom, and are readily exercised when occasion calls. This Job protests to be a part of his own disposition: —

'If I withheld from the poor what they asked,
Or have grieved the eyes of the widow,
Or have eaten my morsel alone,
And the orphan hath not partaken with me;
If from my youth I did not nourish them as a father;
If from my earliest years I was not the widow's guide;
If I have seen any perish for want of clothing,
Or any poor man without raiment.'

"Pursuing an open and ingenuous course, with a conscience unsullied, and a countenance unabashed, Job attempted nothing like concealment of what was passing within his mind. He had nothing to hide, nothing to palliate. He was a living, walking, acting model of integrity, formed upon the reverential fear of God, and a scrupulous regard to his commandments. He offers to subject himself to any infamy or punishment, if his fellow-men could discover in him any delinquency.

'If, human-like, I concealed my sin,
And hid my transgression in my bosom;
Let me be confounded before the multitude;
Let me be covered with public contempt;
Let me be dumb, nor dare to go abroad.'

"He is so entirely confident of the purity and uprightness of his conduct and motives, that he proposes, in language of astonishing boldness and grandeur, to meet the scanning eye of the All-seeing himself, and lay his soul open to his dread inspection. There is neither pride nor arrogance, presumption nor vain-glory, in thus demeaning himself. Self-vindication rendered it necessary, as regarded his fellow-men; and, as regards God, it is only the language of an undaunted child of God appealing to his Father for the sincerity of his affection; an appeal, we may presume, more pleasing than offensive to the Most High.

'O that God would deign to hear me!
This is my declaration: let the Almighty reply to it;
Let my opponent write down the charge:
Surely I would wear it on my shoulder;
I would bind it round me like a diadem;
I would disclose to him the number of my steps;
I would approach him with the boldness of a prince.'

"But without further comment, we may here give a summary of the other branches of morality to which this holy man gave due observance, as we collect them from his own protestations.

"So far was he from neglecting the cause of the poor, and thereby incurring their imprecations, that he had gained their deepest reverence and attachment, as their uniform and steadfast benefactor.

'When the ear heard me, then it blessed me;
When the eye saw me, it gave signs of approbation.
The blessing of him who was perishing came upon me,
And I caused the widow's heart to sing for joy.'

"In his capacity as judge, he discharged his office with undeviating rectitude, and his decisions were fully approved of.

'I put on equity, and clothed myself with it;
My justice was as a robe and a diadem.
I was eyes to the blind;
I was feet to the lame;
I was a father to the destitute;
And I inquired carefully into the cause of the stranger.'

"He was the friend, the protector, and adviser of the widow and the orphan. Chap. xxxi. 16, 17.

"He would not defraud of their wages the laborers who cultivated his land. Chap. xxxi. 39.

"He exercised in its fullest extent the virtue of hospitality.

'The stranger lodged not in the street;
My door was open to every comer.'

The consequence of all which conduct was, that he was received with reverence, affection, and gratitude wherever he went; no one presuming to speak till he had done, to add to what he said, or to suggest anything as being preferable or wiser. They listened patiently to his counsels, they gratefully followed his advice.

'To me men gave ear and attended;
They were silent at my admonition.
After I had spoken they replied not;
For my reasons dropped on them as dew:
They waited for me as for a spring-shower;
They opened wide their mouths, as for the harvest-rain.'

"The young shrank back from the presence of their emir through modesty; the aged rose to meet him from respect. Confident of all this, Job at one time expected to die as he had lived, in calmness and prosperity, reaping the fruits of his piety and rectitude, and seeing his posterity enjoy the advantage of their progenitor's exalted reputation.

'Then I said, I shall die in my nest;
I shall multiply my days as the palm-tree;
My root shall spread out to the waters;
The dew of night shall repose on my branches;
My glory shall be unfading around me,
And my bow continue fresh in my hand.'"

www.ingramcontent.com/pod-product-compliance
Lightning Source LLC
LaVergne TN
LVHW010243110826
845151LV00004B/1373

* 9 7 8 1 4 2 5 5 2 4 0 6 7 *